MOTHER MARIA

Her Life in Letters

Mother Maria

MOTHER MARIA

Her Life in Letters

Selected, edited, and introduced
with a brief biography by
SISTER THEKLA

PAULIST PRESS
New York Ramsey Toronto

First published in the United States by Paulist Press
Editorial Office: 1865 Broadway, N.Y., N.Y. 10023
Business Office: 545 Island Road, Ramsey, N.J. 07446

Published by arrangement with
Darton, Longman & Todd, London

ISBN 0–8091–0286–2

Library of Congress Catalog Card No. 79–63455

Printed in Great Britain

It is only *The Hidden Treasure* I
mind walking about in its beggar's
cloak, as if it were a book and not a
living, wounded life.

CONTENTS

Acknowledgements   viii

Foreword   ix

Introduction   xiii

I   The Communion of Saints   1
Mother of God – saints – martyrs – ubiquity

II   The Mind   8
Bad and good thinking – doubt – philosophy lived – limitation of reason – consent of the mind

III   The Orthodox Faith   24
Platonic attitude – the Mystery – reality of the event – repentance – liturgical texts – Old Testament – tradition – translation

IV   Prayer and Answer   44
Work inside the darkness – love and trust

V   Monasticism   56

VI   Dying to the World   73
Passivity – living – unifying of will – worldly success – values – judgement – teaching

VII   The Work of Love   85
Integration of evil – reality of the person – the centre

VIII   The End-Point   100
The death-country – at the gap – Christ

IX   The Mystery of Death   118

X   Her Writing   126

ACKNOWLEDGEMENTS

We wish to thank Miss Alice Gysi and Father Richard Catterall for their great help in translating German texts of letters.

We also warmly thank the friends who contributed letters and extracts from letters: Prof. A. Hilary Armstrong; Prof. Hans Binder; Mrs Heidi Burchhardt-Vischer; Mrs Irene Cassis; Mrs Kira Clegg; Miss Winifred Clout; Canon Henry Cooper; Pastor Rufus and Marianne Flügge; Mrs Winifred Frohne; Mrs Sheila Gordon-Duff; Dr Werner and Doris Gysi; Mrs Rachel Harding; the Rev. Timothy Hollis; Miss Jo Klaver; Mrs Mary Malley; Father Ralph Martin, s.s.m.; Mr Michael Pimlott; Father Hugh Randolph, o.c.; Mrs Mary Roberts; Mr Paul Stanjer; Mrs Doris Sträuli-Keller; Mrs Mary Wells; Miss Judith Weston; Mrs Martha Woolley.

NOTE

A list of Mother Maria's published works appears on p. 126. Most titles are available in the Library of Orthodox Thinking and can be obtained from booksellers or from the publishers: The Greek Orthodox Monastery of the Assumption, Normanby, Whitby, North Yorkshire, YO22 4PS.

FOREWORD

Wherever possible I have tried to keep to the objectivity of the extracts but, where the meaning might be obscured, I have given a brief reference to the context. A (G) at the end of an extract or following the date of a letter indicates a German original. I have also given some cross-references to a few passages as a hint to the dynamic of Mother Maria's thinking: always following the need of the person, according to the demand, yet never relative. I have arranged the letters in a certain order, yet, as there was never in Mother's life any system of ideology, so there is no *system* of life to be deduced from this arrangement. Its purpose merely is to give some guideline for the journey through her life in letters: I have begun with heaven, the reality of the saints; and then through the reality of heaven incarnate on earth, the road leads to the listening to God, and so to the great dialectic of the Christian soul: dying to the world that we might work in the world. Only in death, the world becomes the field of activity for the one work necessary: the work of love. This is the work which alone is essentially active, for it allows no room for re-action. The seat of the work of love, in every soul, is the centre, the mystery of the innermost being in its reality as fashioned by God in the beginning. So the journey reaches its end-point, the gap before death, into the country of death, and to the incomprehensible heaven. The journey might be seen as a circle, and I think that this might please Mother Maria for there is no hint, nor place, in such a circle, for any ladder of perfection.

As will be seen, there are to be found in the letters, as in Mother Maria's books, some unusual constructions and uncommon word-forms. Such unconventional usage reflects much of the living dialectic of her thought. There is also a consistent use of certain terms which may not be self-evident at first sight. *Doubt* is not confined to the sphere of religion, but covers the inner cleavage before any problem: *double ignorance* specifically refers to the conviction of one's knowledge when one does not know. The *middle sphere* is the part in man most actively concerned in all the troubles and demands and pleasures of the world: it is the part which *re-acts*, what sometimes Mother refers to as the 'frills'. It is all that, and more, which falls into the sphere of psychology. *Transfiguration* is even technically used as seeing a person or situation in its *reality*, normally hidden from us or not discerned by us. *Reality* is the innermost core of purity as given by God in the beginning without the hundreds of overlaid fringes. *Love* is always the meeting of the other in his *reality*, where people are concerned, and the not turning aside to any pull of evil. Love is the immutable self-orientation on to the transcendent. *Evil* is not just obvious *bad*, but all the parasite growths in their many disguises to divert the soul from the unifying work of love.

Dialectic is the key to so much and as Mother once explained it herself in a letter to Sister Katherine on March 23rd, 1967, it seems advisable to insert this extract here on the *double crossing-out*.

The Double Crossing-out[1]

Think of Thesis – Antithesis – Synthesis.

In the antithesis, the thesis is crossed out, and in the synthesis both thesis and antithesis are:

1) Crossed out in their idiosyncratic form.
2) Preserved in their lasting essence.
3) Lifted up to a higher dimension – from which a new dialectic process can start.

One must think of it in a living way, as a *living* process: the thesis giving itself to the antithesis and the synthesis being desired by both. (St Catherine: the soul throwing itself into purgatory.) It is the *living* thinking, where no assertion is held in its own undoubted way *against* any other: a thinking which will grasp the 'other', digest it, find eagerly its essence and

[1] cf. II, October 24th, 1973 (p. 19)

has therefore to die into it – and then rise out of it to a new form.

In a less logical way, you can think of pain and joy being linked, crossed out and lifted into a new entity, where both *are* still, yet both are gone as separate parts. This is really the exact description of dialectic thinking.

To make it clear, if one loses the thread, is the first pre- mise, that nothing is ever shut out. It cannot be shut out of the mind of God; so we come nearest, if we take in what comes into our grasp and digest it as best we can into the context of our present thought.

Instead of representing it as a linear *process*, rather more subtle and accurate, one can say the same thing in this way:

1) We have a certain conscious content of thought; a relation- ship of ideas at every moment changing.
2) A new experience rouses new aspects or ideas.
3) The new idea has to be worked into the former relation- ship.
4) A new content is formed and that implies a modification both of the previous content and the new, taken-in idea.
5) Thought lovingly, this means, of the old the loving receiving of the new and sacrifice of the old in self- surrender to truth, if, perchance, truth will come of it; and from the new idea an acceptance to enter into union with a context of ideas.
6) Out comes a mind, which is *alive*, never asserting itself as autonomous entity, as immutable knowledge, but hum- bly yielding to new knowledge, however much effort this demands.

This actually implies a *constant dying* of the mind, a constant refinding of new life; and a never sitting still on any 'find', ever knocking, ever asking.

Event and significance
The dying and self-sacrifice of the 'event': it also implies a sacrifice of the idea, when entering into the event (a sort of incarnation) and then rising after its death in the event, as enriched meaning. If the event is left out, one lands at the other end on a flat plane of logic (ultimately). It is *bad* ration-

alism and childish confidence in our capacity to discard the
event, which in very many ways may lead to ever new
significance; whereas, if it is discarded, only *one* significance
ensues and this one statically; it does not live. It is extracted,
*ab*stracted from life.

This is actually the principle of dialectic thinking. Where
the mistake comes in is again in a transgression of our limits,
when Hegel proclaims that 'the Spirit' is thinking in us and
goes its journey through finite minds (later Marxism),
sacrificing the *persons* to the idea and the event. It is quite a
different matter to think of the self-sacrifice of person and
event into a new person and event, more 'real' than the
former.

INTRODUCTION

The life and the death of Mother Maria, her books, and her letters, are all of one piece. From childhood to death she remained consistent to the single vision: the tender love of God.

It is perhaps, therefore, not surprising that the facts of her life may well seem unimportant in themselves, or even misleading, because the facts, *in themselves*, can only suggest an inadequate expression of the spirit which lived in them and through them. This will become clear in her letters. But it is enough here to remember that, throughout her life, she never conceded to outside events the honour of any autonomous power. Yet, equally, she gladly welcomed every outside event as the food for the work of the spirit. So it is perhaps best to follow the outward sequence of her life as a gradually unfolding map which, when we have finished, remains the one map. And that we might glimpse something of her inside the context of the world, I shall try to trace the way briefly from birth until death.

The First Years (1912–32)

Mother Maria was born in Basle on May 14th, 1912. Her parents, Ernst and Martha Gysi, traced themselves back for many generations of strongly respectable Swiss stock: squires and peasants, but including, to Mother's delight, a professional jester! Her parents already had two daughters, Martha and Alice, but the girl-infant, five years younger than Alice, was greeted with tender welcome.

Ernst Gysi was a schoolmaster, particularly concerned with backward children. It was a happy family, enjoying its own fun, but strictly and correctly Methodist. Thus, our future Orthodox abbess was duly baptized Lydia in the

xiii

Methodist chapel on June 16th, 1912. As a little girl, Lydia
was taken regularly to this chapel where her father held a
respected position amongst the largely artisan congregation.
She was still very young when she demanded to sit with the
'brothers', considering the 'sisters' less interesting compan-
ions. And, at this stage, she once 'witnessed' with such moving pathos that the whole congregation was deeply impressed
and congratulated her father on such piety in his youngest
child. Yet, even at the age of six or seven, something in her
was yearning for a beauty beyond her horizon and, ignoring
any possible restriction, she crept out one evening to glimpse
the forbidden Carnival in the streets of Basle, and so caught
her first vision of glory in the guise of a pierrot. To the end of
her life she felt that she had missed the ordinary social gaiety
of childhood and insisted that when she died the first thing
heaven would teach her would be how to dance!

It was from these first years that Mother Maria learned the
spontaneous hospitality, although the family was far from
rich, to all who came, with no fuss of preparation. In the
early monastic years at Filgrave, with the coming of unexpected visitors, Mother Maria, true to her upbringing,
serenely insisted that in our monastery people would always
be welcomed, whenever and however they came, and that
cooking and cleaning were a mere 'matter for the left hand',
whilst the right remained free for the real work of love. She
faithfully kept this precept to the end, somehow relegating
her last long illness to a mere 'matter for the left hand', while
her right hand sovereignly welcomed every demand.

What else of those first years? We know that she swam in
the river with other children, that she learned to sew, rode on
her father's shoulders pulling his hair, and had a small spade
to help him with his vegetables. There were visits to her
loved Aunt Fanni who allowed her to rummage to her heart's
content in high chests of drawers. To the pre-school days
belong her daily visits to her father's school. She was given
her own little chair to sit on at the back of his class and here
she occupied herself in sewing, knitting, drawing, absorbed
in peaceful recollection. She was apparently the object of
deepest veneration on the part of the small and backward
boys, and one actually dared to approach her with the gift of

two beautifully coloured peacock feathers, but in spite of severe temptation she thought it proper only to accept one. At the age of seven, the normal age for school entry in Switzerland, in April 1919 Lydia Gysi entered primary school. One gathers that she was not very happy there, for some time being not well treated by a Roman Catholic teacher, but after four years, at the age of eleven, she transferred to the Girls' Gymnasium of Basle and life, until the age of fourteen, continued on its happily sober way.

During holidays there were the expeditions up the mountains, starting before dawn. Lydia did not long suffer the humiliation of returning by train with her mother but pursued her father and sisters, to walk as an equal with them. There was bread and chocolate to eat and milk to drink in the Alpine huts; and pure, Swiss air. There were the rushing mountain brooks, quite unlike what she chose to call the English 'stagnant rivers'. And tourists to laugh at: you could always tell the English by the amount of their luggage! But one knew the places where tourists did not penetrate.

Then, throughout the years, there were the visits from cousins, the elder boys much admired. There were visits from relations as far-flung as the childless couple from America who offered to adopt Lydia and give her a wealthy home. There were big Methodist conferences whose delegates were welcomed in their home. And there was the weekly washing in the huge copper in the cellar, the three sisters helping. In fact, all the ordinary joys and tragedies of childhood. At the age of ten, Lydia began violin lessons and she continued to play for many years, giving, as she said, herself pleasure if not reaching a professional standard. She was, however, invited even during her schooldays to play publicly with orchestras, although she was made to sit with her face averted so that no one might witness the faces she pulled in concentration. Up to the age of thirteen or fourteen she read very little, always loving books, sitting amongst them and listening, delicately touching them, but withholding from entry into their mystery. Perhaps she was waiting for the exact moment to come.

The tranquil security of the first years was rudely broken by her father's long illness, beginning about the time Lydia was fourteen. From now on, the family lived constantly under the cloud of anxiety, behaving as normally as they could, but home was not as stable as it had been and more responsibility fell upon the three daughters. At school, Lydia in the lower forms was a quiet pupil, keeping her place, with what seemed unexpected bursts of brilliance. But in the higher forms her intellectual capacities became more apparent, particularly in literature. In Switzerland, school continued until the twentieth year, so, in common with her contemporaries, in her last year Lydia was growing restless. She has confessed to knitting through the French lessons, and to displaying such boredom during one geography lesson that the geography master suggested that she might care to take over the lesson herself. For once forgetting her shyness, she did take over the lesson with such intelligent aplomb that at the end he sincerely congratulated her on her pedagogic ability! But she was not destined for a teacher. Lydia matriculated and left school with the highest honour: she was chosen to make the leaving speech on the last day. This was in April 1932.

Nursing (1932–43)

In her last years at school, Lydia had already made student friends, some older than herself. She was introduced into lives less overtly narrow than her own, and, in particular, had met her first Russian influence, both in the avid reading of Dostoievsky, and in the person of Robert Crottet, then a young author. Through him she would meet in 1935 Father Dimitri, as yet a student, and the whole pattern of her religious life would have its inceptive design. In the course of her life she was only to meet Father Dimitri on six brief occasions, but he remained, as he began, the 'person' for her of the Orthodox faith. Looking back at herself at this period, she wrote in September 1975:

> ... When I was twenty I decided to discover God in my own way, first by disregarding all the Judgement-images, and by only accepting him as love with no limit in every, even the merely earthly, sense and image; and in the fain-

test reflection of love, I would find him in his 'beggar's cloak' – and the end of the journey brought me to the beginning of a faith fulfilled in the same blindness.

But, in the meantime, on the practical level, which way to go? Lydia had seriously considered a medical career, but her father's illness and perhaps some inner resistance of her own to so final a commitment, held her back from the long and expensive training, and she chose nursing, as a kind of short-cut to sick people, entering the Nurses' Training School in Zürich in 1932, and qualifying with the General Nurses' Diploma at the end of 1935. Her memories of her training years varied: sometimes of mischief, as when she and a friend, tired of an autocratic Sister's reiterated homilies on cleanliness, in mute reproach day after day emptied the whole medicine cupboard, scrubbed the shelves, and returned every bottle to its place meticulously washed. The Sister, a zealous exponent of the Protestant deaconess 'vocation' tradition in the Zürich Hospital which she, rightly, suspected Lydia of not respecting in the letter of the law, retained her self-dignity by confiding her concern for Sister Lydia's general clumsiness and stupidity. Yet the moments of fun were rare. Mostly Mother Maria's memories have been of dread: of wards endlessly long, of weak voices calling and only herself on lonely night duty to answer, of running backwards and forwards, and of watching alone in the dreaded hours before dawn when life so often slipped away. She felt so young and inadequate to face these vigils with death, yet there grew in her the strange conviction that it was precisely her work in helping others to die: to show the peace of the end. We know how the patients loved her and were soothed by this young girl's presence. Anyone sick in her care will have experienced the mystery of her healing power: not of making well directly, but of taking away the inner pain of reproach or fear or impatience, and somehow turning the illness into a blessing sent by God.

After qualifying, Lydia left Zürich in 1936 and moved to Paris, having found work in the American hospital in Neuilly, where she numbered among her patients a spoiled American film star who bestowed on her unwanted gifts from an elderly lover. Lydia stood no nonsense from her, and nursed her as gently as she would one of her dying tramps in Zürich. In 1937 she found her first Russian 'home' with Mother Maria (Skobtsova). It was in the chapel of rue Lourmel that Lydia, on June 7th, 1937 was received into the Orthodox Church with all Father Lev's sympathetic understanding of her individual way. And the young and befriended Lydia listened eagerly to the conversations of Mother Maria with some of the best minds of the Russian *émigré* world in Paris. She drank in the whole Russian Orthodox spirit, its warmth and its openness, and she attended frequent Liturgies, nourishment for years to come. The fleas and the dirt, Mother Maria's vehement rejection of traditional monasticism, the smell of soup, all had for Lydia the fragrance of freedom, of minds compassionate and alert. It was during this time in Paris with Russians who kept their pre-revolution dynamic of thinking, that Lydia absorbed *natural* Orthodoxy, on which she was later to found her own monastery, and which she embodied in her writings: an Orthodoxy that sees no necessity to defend itself either by barriers, or by constant apologia vis-à-vis the West.

Lydia, who as a child had slipped out to see the Carnival, now walked fearlessly through the streets of Paris at night, returning home late after a Vigil Service. Sometimes, when she was followed, she would let her would-be assailant catch up with her and talk to him as an equal and a friend until he left her. One street youth told her that she need never fear: she was safe to venture anywhere alone. But he could not explain the reason; he just knew. He said something about its being the expression of her eyes. He was quite right, of course: wherever she has been, there has never been any effort to molest her. And she herself never felt any fear, except once, when she was in no danger at all as a Swiss citizen, but it was in an interview at a police-station in occupied France, face to face with a Nazi policeman. She felt herself at the point of fainting, through the sheer physical impact of evil.

All this was as far from Protestant Basle as her twenty-five-year-old heart could have wished. But she was a serious nurse and returned to Basle in 1938 to take her midwifery course, still with some idea of missionary work – perhaps to join Albert Schweitzer, whom she had met and who had encouraged her vocation. But the war came.

At first Lydia worked as a midwife, mainly in Zürich under military direction. Then she was at home to nurse her father until his death in 1942, when she joined the Red Cross and was sent as midwife to the south of France, to work in the unit assigned for expectant mothers (Spanish and Jewish) in the vicinity of the concentration camp. So began the nightmare time. It is the story we all know only too well: babies born to emaciated mothers; no food, no drugs, no proper medical aid; babies weaned with nothing to wean them on; babies with old faces, dying as she watched help-lessly. And a few yards away was the agony of thousands, the mute suffering of the doomed, the departures at night to nowhere. For years afterwards, Lydia could hardly bear to eat without instinctively hiding the food to take back to the starving. I think that it was in this agony that her attitude to *numbers* grew. She once told me never to forget that each person only dies once. This was no means of escape from the pain of compassion, but, rather, the reverse; for this realiza-tion takes away the ease of generalized horror and concen-trates all the force of compassion on to the one person, whom our imagination can grasp without dispersing, as it does when faced by impersonally large numbers. I think that later she was to apply the same principle to its contradiction of success. She could never see why large numbers should so awaken popular appraisal except again in the non-comprehending of the person; and, again, as indifferent in approval as in horror.

Somehow, I do not know the details, Lydia did become a little involved with the underground movement, and she cer-tainly needed to visit a 'house without doors', and was con-cerned in getting somebody over the border into Spain. I think it was this man's sister, a somewhat eccentric woman who poured wisdom upon her and made outrageous demands on her service, but who yet turned Lydia's thoughts seriously to academic study. She certainly had some form of persecution mania, perhaps not unfounded, and she again and again sent Lydia in search of obscure farms where she could live safely for a short time. But during all this, it was she, with all her impossibility, who first not only recognized Lydia's mind, but insisted that it would be the blackest betrayal on her part not to study. Other reasons necessitated leaving France, and so in 1943, Lydia returned to Switzerland, now, at last, for the explicit work of the mind.

The Study Years (1944–50)

In order to enter the theological faculty of Basle University, it was necessary to matriculate in Hebrew and Greek. This Lydia achieved concurrently by intensive study within nine months, gaining the highest mark of 6 in Hebrew and 5½ in Greek. She was then admitted into the University in 1944.

Mother Maria used to say, in later years, that she confirmed her Orthodox faith by the close study of Protestant theology and she certainly had the most thorough 'reformed' curriculum of study on all aspects of history of religion, comparative religions, and even in her final year, seminars involving the writing of sermons. But here there was some misunderstanding, for what she produced did not strike the lecturer as in any way conforming to the required pattern. However, she pleaded the truth: 'But I am Orthodox.' The theology time ended with the completion of the required qualifying examination, yet during this time nothing had been wasted, for she studied Old Testament under Professor Walter Baumgartner, who gave her the way of exegesis into the Bible which she retained all her life. The prophets, men and women of old Israel, the psalms, all lived for her now as *people* and the writings of real people, under the loving care of a God who was always near, and to whom they talked, and complained, and with whom they pleaded and rejoiced. Professor Baumgartner encouraged Lydia in original research, respecting her dislike for secondary sources, and his guidance led her to 'chase the Devil through the New Testament', to come out in 1947 with the treatise which was later to turn into *Evil in the New Testament*.

In 1945, Lydia privately began her philosophy studies concurrently with theology, although she did not transfer to the Philosophical Faculty until the autumn of 1947. All that had come earlier seems to have led to this point, and all that came later follows from this point of the first meeting with Hermann Gauss, the Platonist. It was as if in Gauss Lydia met her *Staretz*, and he his disciple in her. The grey cloak which she always wore, he recognized as her monastic enclosure inside the world. It was his hope to take the next step from Plato into the Gospel, but he did not live to take this step. His spark kindled in Lydia, and it is as if she were to live what he had taught, but first came years of intensive study. On November 24th, 1945 she wrote of the beginning:

I have the great joy to be allowed to work one hour a week in private with one of our philosophers [Dr. Gauss], i.e. he takes me through the history of philosophy. The hours are fine, like journeys to the stars, always to the boundaries of thought. But I have to work hard for it.... These philosophy hours are a wholly unique experience: out of my agitated living into the perfect clarity and stillness of thought, where one becomes aware that creative power comes out of the stillness, but a stillness so profound, so absolute. Every time I think: if only the hour could last all the week!

I believe there is nothing in the world more wonderful than people who carry this stillness inside themselves like a wide sea. There streams out from them a sheltering which has no limits or barriers. There one has space and is allowed to grow. (G).

We will meet the *boundaries of thought* as the sure foundation for thinking, repeatedly and urgently, in all Mother Maria's work to come.

To begin with, Lydia lived at home but after a time she rented a small room, her *réduit*, where she could work and sleep without disturbing anyone. Sometimes she hardly slept for days, and after a particular piece of writing had been accomplished, she would sleep literally for days. Her health certainly suffered in those years of intensive mental work and physical strain, but her mind and her spirit flourished and blossomed in the light of Reason which she had sought so long. Mind and heart were at one in Platonic thought and

Orthodox faith, not merely the mind in the philosophy and the faith in the religion, but both in each. In 1946 she wrote:

> While in Preles, I swallowed the whole of Descartes, so to speak – in one go, and now I am chewing him. It is always the same, I simply have to give myself to a philosopher with my whole being, without any reserve, and slowly creep away from him again. Not a bad way, but certainly somewhat exhausting. (G).

In consultation with Gauss, who directed her doctoral thesis, the decision was taken that the thesis should be on the Cambridge Platonists; in particular, Cudworth. This meant finally the necessity to come to England, where certain documents were only available in the British Museum. So in 1949 Lydia came to England, shy, uncertain of colloquial English but proficient in the seventeenth century, and friendless. She found her temporary home at the Fellowship of St Alban and St Sergius in Ladbroke Grove, and there she settled in the basement, with the chapel above her head. Her life took on a pattern: studying most of the day, and praying at night, with the inner monastic direction growing stronger. Unlike the days with Mother Maria Skobtsova in the rue Lourmel, the time in St Basil's was indeed lonely. Not only was she too immersed in work to seek friendship, but she found none of the spontaneous friendliness towards the unknown stranger amongst the English and the English-Russian which she had met in the Russians of France, and she was too unworldly to break through the more formal behaviour herself. Her practical problem was food, particularly in post-war London. She did not have much money, nor the facilities nor time for anything but the simplest cooking. She shopped in the Portobello Road, and there at the grocer's, she longed for an egg. Each week she asked for one, and each week monotonously she was told, 'for regular customers only'. Exhausted with study and lack of sleep, one week her courage broke, and gently through her tears she asked the simple question: 'But how does one *become* a regular customer?' The manager, summoned to the scene of distress, at once produced six eggs, and she was never again refused. It was so exactly her in the whole course of her life, not to complain, nor demand her rights, but in full trust to question the one principle involved.

The thesis was completed, and Lydia returned to Switzerland for its presentation and approval in September 1950: Lydia Gysi: *Platonism and Cartesianism in the Philosophy of Ralph Cudworth* (published by Herbert Lang, Bern, in English in 1962). The approval was conditional on the oral examination, an occasion for intensive mental concentration which ended in her receiving her doctorate *cum laude*. The official studies were over. Again the question, what next? The obvious way would have been the academic, yet this was not her choice. The inner pull, more and more, was towards the monastic life, active, as she thought then, something on the pattern of Mother Maria Skobtsova, some form of social or parish work. She returned to England with this in mind.

The Abbey Years (1951–65)

Inwardly, Lydia's vocation was clear. But where? There was no Orthodox monastery in England. The predicament was temporarily solved in 1951 by Father Anthony now Metropolitan Anthony of Sourozh. He knew and respected Mother Mary, Abbess of the Anglican Benedictine Community at St Mary's Abbey, West Malling, and he approached her to take in Lydia. After some hesitation Mother Mary agreed to admit her, already clothed, but not yet professed, by Father Anthony, to follow the normal training of a novice with the intention that at the end of two years she would leave to begin some work which would by then have materialized. It was agreed that she should leave the enclosure regularly to go to London for Confession and Liturgies. So Sister Lydia arrived in West Malling and her whole energy awoke to flow into the stream of silence. Her hidden years merged naturally into the Benedictine Rule, which after the years of study, of nervous strain, and unknown future, richly fed her soul. She wrote to a schoolfriend on January 5th, 1953:

It is something wonderful to learn to know a tradition so in its own heart, and to live with it; a true ecumenical work. But the Benedictines are a world to themselves, and one can hardly think of anything on earth more beautiful and wide. (G).

She never forgot the strong, silent rhythm of the Benedictine Rule, and referred to it again and again in the course of her life, and in her writing. I think she was most struck by how the Rule allowed the freedom to the personal spiritual growth, while protecting on the psychological level from oneself as well as others. With the careful forbidding of any kind of mutual intrusion or private inquiring into each other, the Rule allowed for the solitude of the desert within the balance of community life, and, as it were, the 'carrying power' for the weaker ones in body or spirit. But from the point of view of the future, most important of course was her meeting with Sister Katherine,[1] then her Novice Mistress. It was not long before the work together began which did not cease until Mother Maria's death, and continues now. Sister Lydia's seventeenth-century English was fluent, but her colloquial or modern English was still a little hesitant, and at the experimental stage. She was very fond always of 'trying out' words. It was Sister Katherine who gently restrained her from 'trying out' the *dentures of the lion* as a possible alternative to the *lion's teeth* in the translation of the Psalms. Without Sister Katherine the phenomenal writing output of the Abbey years would have been severely hampered. She helped consistently, as far as her duties allowed, with her peculiar grace for corresponding melody.

Most of Mother Maria's writing in the Abbey was directed primarily to the community. She wanted to share all that was hers. So came *The Loneliness of God's Saints* and *The Two Temples* already in 1951, in 1954 the original of the *Introduction to the Divine Liturgy*, and so too in 1954 the work on the prophet Jeremiah (still unpublished), the translation of the poems, and the stories of his life sent daily in instalments to Sister Katherine who was in hospital. In 1955 the translation of the Psalms was in process of completion, and more or less concurrently the work on Genesis (also as yet unpublished).

[1] then Dame Mary Thomas

1956 saw *The Jesus Prayer* in its first form as talks to the community, 1959 *The Hidden Treasure* and 1960 *The Sceptrum Regale*, and the Isaiah translations (also unpublished) almost completed. This could never have been achieved except in the total concentration possible in silence. And it must be remembered that Mother Maria did not only spend her days in writing. Much of her time was spent in the workroom, sewing and mending, and washing. She introduced, with the ultimate Swiss cleanliness fostered in the nursing years, an intensified system of blanket and habit washing. She also inspired others to sew, as she did: following the material in its plastic nature in a rhythmic harmony. We often laughed in the Filgrave days and accused her of 'cleaning the wards again', but never in my life have I met such graceful move-ment of cleaning: Mother Maria, mop, floor, all one, in a gracious sweep of obedience to the truth of cleanliness. I think she suffered a good deal quietly at our jabbing efforts to clean round her when she was in bed in the last days, but she always only thanked us so sweetly, fearful of what she saw as extra work for us.

The anticipated two years imperceptibly merged into three, five, seven and still Sister Lydia was at the Abbey and to all appearances would remain there for the rest of her life. So in 1958, on September 24th, Bishop Anthony professed her in the Abbey chapel as the Nun Maria before a large congregation of Anglicans and Orthodox, and for the first time the Abbey nuns were present on the next day at an Orthodox Liturgy. In fact some of them participated, Sister Lydia having taught them to sing the Profession Service. Now she was Mother Maria, a professed Orthodox nun in the Russian jurisdiction, but still she remained in the Abbey. The time was not yet for her to leave. In all the routine of Abbey life, sometimes she felt only one loss, or, at least, a temporary allaying, and that was the purely philosophical sharpness of thought. In these years the emphasis was rather on the spirit than on the mind *as* mind. Part of her was undoubtedly a little hungry when Professor Jaeger appeared, demanding her collaboration on the Cambridge Platonists in the book he was producing on the Reformed Churches. If she was a little hungry, from now on she had no cause to complain of undernourishment. She was inundated from 1963 by requests for selection of texts, translation into German, notes of textual criticism, research into sources. It was an avalanche into her secluded life. At the moment of my appearance, she was in the worst work-fever, which in fact did not abate until after 1966. The book finally appeared in three volumes, and the third volume on the Anglican Church in which Mother Maria is acknowledged as collaborator was published in 1972 by Mathias-Grünewald, under the title *Zeugnis für die Einheit*. Such was the burden of translation and retranslation that I well remember in Filgrave when we were translating the Herbert Essay, which she wrote in German, into English, for one second we were both convinced that we must translate the quoted texts from Herbert as well as her writing!

Instead of the stipulated two, fourteen years had passed. It was August 1965 and Mother Maria was in the throes of the Anglican text work. On Sunday August 15th, the Western Assumption (we used the Old Style in the Russian Church), Mother Maria went up to the Liturgy in Ennismore Gardens, and I also went because there was no service that day in Oxford. So I saw Mother for the first time, a glimpse as she walked away from Confession, but a glimpse which not only changed the trend of my life, but brought her out of the Abbey, to the open ministry which she always knew she must face before death.

Filgrave (1965–74)

On Monday August 16th, 1965 I went down to Kent, to St Mary's Abbey, for a few days of 'rest'. I wanted to be quiet, and I was not particularly pleased at being invited to the parlour to meet an Orthodox nun. I can see that parlour so clearly: the little room, a clock busily ticking, and a table with a chair on one side by the enclosure door and a chair on the other by the entrance door. The enclosure door opened, and her smile lit the room as her smile always would. Radiant, as always in times of stress, she declared, 'I am *drowning* in work', and, as it were for good measure, 'I am a Platonist.' But I only said, 'Oh, it's *you*.' And so, in that formal parlour our monastery was born. The call had come for which she had waited, and which she had dreaded but would never deny.

As the old Abbess Mary had accepted Mother, so now her successor, the Abbess Osyth, and the Sisters, dearly welcomed the second Orthodox intrusion. As soon as the situation was recognized by all, it was the Abbey which made Filgrave a reality and not a dream. On April 22nd, 1966, Mother wrote to Doris Keller, a close friend in Switzerland:

Since last autumn my life has been one single great movement to the late summer, when we shall have our own little monastery, which the Abbey has given us. The call came with such strong inner evidence, that it was easy to follow in spite of the pains of separation. All is now in the process of development, and it is difficult to say anything of the new, the lines of which only now begin to appear, and yet which from day to day takes shape and grows inwardly. (G).

The Abbey gave Mother the money to buy the house and paid for the building, but even more, it was the Abbey which upheld us in our monastic integrity. The Abbey assumed for us the solidity of a 'Mother-House'. In November, my half-term, we found the house; and in December, just after Christmas, Metropolitan Anthony clothed me at the Abbey, with the Sisters present as they had been at Mother's profession. I went on teaching in the months that followed, going to the Abbey as often as I could, changing into my habit in the car, and creeping into the silent enclosure. Mother, still under the pressure of the Anglican text work, supervised the building at Filgrave, and in all the upheaval quietly began to direct my thought to a reasonable attitude of mind. She first introduced me to Plato's Ideas when, on our way to the Abbey one Friday evening, we were held up in a traffic block for over an hour. It was the dreariest bit of road possible, and there I understood for the first time the imperfection of any human achievement, even in relation to the idea as conceived in the mind.

I left teaching in July 1966, and went to the Abbey. The intention was that I should have a 'retreat' to begin my full-time monastic life, but this was not to be. On July 18th, the police telephoned from Newport Pagnell that there had been a burglary of copper pipes and that we had better come. So we went, arriving at midnight. Of course we were frightened: there were no outside doors, the rooms were more or less uninhabitable, there was no electricity and no heating. And there was the possibility of the thieves returning to complete their haul. There were mice everywhere, and the question of rats. We slept on mattresses and prayed at night, when the men had gone, by the light of paraffin lamps. And in the midst of the dust and the dirt and all the uncertainties, Mother tranquilly opened my eyes to the Old Testament, of which I knew nothing, and to the Gospels in all the richness of real presence. I also met St Paul for the first time out of the context of dogmatic distortion. And all this seemed to come without the least emphasis of training or teaching, but ever as the answer to eager questioning. Of these first few months, Mother wrote again to Doris Keller on December 19th, 1966:

> We walked through months of the most difficult outward conditions of life. No light, an army of mice, no hot water, endless holes in the walls, cold – but one after the other is now resolved and our beloved house looks solid and true, with a special beauty. The walls are white, windows and doors stained in dark brown. We are just arranging the chapel, and we have all the pains of decisions. At midnight I think, tired to death, in my bed, and writing is only possible in my mind. (G)

And *how* Mother worked physically. The nettles in the spinney were her particular field of action, as were the bullocks in the next field who insisted on nibbling our fence. How Mother loved the spinney! Once again she wrote to Doris Keller, in 1968:

> I discover only now what it means to live with trees; such great shapes and such multiform 'souls'. There hang the last golden leaves on the branches: tomorrow there will be none; and so many buds already on them all, and the spring babies have already many small leaves. One apple

tree has no more leaves, but ten little golden apples very high, which the birds are enjoying. As last year, a big crow has moved into its winter seat, and is sitting there like a grim professor, turned in on himself and despising the world. (G).

I once found her surrounded by a circle of bullocks intently listening to her sermon on their iniquities. To deter them, we put up barbed wire along the whole perimeter of the fence, the roll balanced on a wheelbarrow. Our courage nearly failed us, but we kept up our spirits by singing 'Onward, Christian Soldiers'! The blue clay in the vegetable patch was another enemy, and so too my blissful ignorance about vegetables: having put in some Brussels Sprout plants I waited for the sprouts to sprout at the top, until Mother suggested that they might come from the sides. We were also infested by rabbits until we wired the patch. I remember that we sent our first three potatoes to the Abbey. The mischief in Mother was always there, gaily surmounting all difficulties as a loving joke on heaven's part. Once we were very short of money for the shopping and she produced about £20. All through my teaching months I had given her money so that she could travel first class and take taxis across London, and she had travelled second and by tube, and now very proudly saved the situation! On November 8th, 1966 Mother passed her driving test first time; and on November 11th the electricity was connected.

So passed four years of comparative silence and retreat. With all the work outside, we achieved a great deal of the work inside for which the Abbey had paved the way by giving us the house. It was their hope that the house would give Mother the opportunity for writing and we, in those years, ordered and revised much that had been written previously in the Abbey. There was also a great deal of translation and retranslation of German writing, and we began on the translation of the services into English from Slavonic.

Mother always knew that the 'opening' must come. She saw it as connected with some catastrophe, not of course foreseeing that it would be her own illness. She wrote to Sister Katherine on January 19th, 1967:

There is a part of me which desires to put up for this last bit of my life no barriers at all; which wants to thrust open all gates and doors to ALL, with no consideration for spiritual life. But obviously I cannot do this; but I believe one day it will come to it, perhaps through a war, for the last days.... I have deep inside passed a frontier into a beyond, where there is (on the deepest level) a strange kind of indifference and openness to ALL – also to all things.

And five months later she wrote to Professor A. H. Armstrong something of her inner distress:

Where shall I begin? Living in four or five different cultures, Churches, Traditions, a-supertraditional in myself – how can I write? I can BE, but write? What is needed? Can it be expressed? I live on too many levels, and when practical things come as well.... Somehow the practical merges – or takes on spiritual, mental value in this condition of super-alertness; together with the *pereat mundus*.... I seem chiefly to be accused in life for having a mind and by every possible contrivance motioned to deny it. But opposition or ridicule never does me any harm, except that it makes one mute and turn to heaven and delight in getting old, wherein I chiefly see the delightful permission of taking the *regnum mundi* no more quite so seriously.

A year later, on December 2nd, 1968, she wrote again:

And every time I am just absorbed and settling to what the house was given us for than a violent interruption comes from outside; and I have to go through days and nights of extraneous anguish of decisions, which I cannot take, because I cannot decide; I can only follow the inner track. I am *not* an Abbess, but a hermit; I kept to the line faithfully from the start. I am an absolute fool in so-called pastoral work. All know it, and yet want to push me into it. So I fight the battles inward of fear, doubt, doubt, fear, till I am quite distracted till the solution is clear. Sometimes I feel, I had better play the fool properly – since this is a revered

Orthodox Tradition!! It is quite nice to have this possibility up one's sleeve.

Her inner distress was often acute, tearing her very being, but outwardly she was always there, ready, a rock of transfiguring strength, shielding me to her uttermost power so that I too might have at least the inner silence, if not the outer solidity, in which her early monastic days were nurtured. As long as she was there, the inner silence was safe whatever the outside situation. Strength, as it were, radiated from her, without her even noticing. Where she was, there was *light*, but she herself only felt the weight of weariness and darkness and responsibility. So we came to 1970, and in 1970 there was once again upheaval. It was only then that, retrospectively, what we had gone through was comparatively a time of peace!

In April 1970, the Russian Patriarch Alexei died. With his death it seemed as if the last tie with old Russia was severed. The future of the Monastery, if there were to be a future, was in England, with English-speaking visitors, and English or English-speaking nuns. Politically we had no affinity with Russia, and now we knew that, for the sake of the Monastery, we must pull up our cherished roots, and transfer intact our *tradition* but not our *expression* into a non-national jurisdiction.

So we sought admission for the Monastery into the Ecumenical Patriarchate. Such a request, if granted, would bring revolution into our quiet life, for it would open the doors to the Greek world. And it was precisely at this moment that the Mother of God, in a blinding vision, told Sister Katherine that she must leave the Abbey, after thirty-three years of enclosed monastic life, and join us, becoming Orthodox. She could not account for this certain knowledge that she must go, nor could we, until the publishing and sickness and death followed which would have foundered us alone, and which no one but Sister Katherine could have shared in carrying. Obviously her announcement came as a severe blow in the Abbey and efforts were made to dissuade her. And she did not come to us until July 1971, just in time to get the bulk of the publishing through before Mother was too ill to bless and

xxxii

guide the enterprise. The year 1970 to 1971 was one of black terror for us: between two Church jurisdictions and isolated from Sister Katherine. We were, indeed, alone. But it was in the late spring that Mother wrote her talk on Eastern Spirituality which she gave in the library of Westminster Cathedral. It was as if the explicit faith of our Church became more and more real in sharpness of outline during the months when on earth it seemed to have left us.

On July 14th, 1971 Sister Katherine came to us, and within days the Monastery was admitted into the Ecumenical Patriarchate. On November 10th Archbishop Athenagoras visited us. He received Sister Katherine into the Orthodox Church, and we were professed together. Mother was announced as Abbess, and the Constitutions of the Monastery were signed. So, once again, we were on an even keel ecclesiastically. And Mother wrote to Professor Armstrong on November 16th:

I already – with the peace – begin to feel that I have 'time' again. Time that I never had for six years. 'Time' is so little connected with actual work. It is something quite different, I believe. It is the absence, or relative absence of pressure on the mind. But, once again, I had to go to the uttermost limit, before the relief came.

And to Mary Malley, in Australia, a friend of many years, she wrote three months later:

The transition into the Greek world from the Russian was exceedingly painful and linked with much anguish, but I believe we are finding firmer ground at least in ourselves.... Let's be brave! Soon the journey will at last come to its end and consummation and what really makes sense come into sight.

Of these first months of opening out, she wrote in December 1971:

Where, where, where have I got to? Who am I? And today came the dear visit of a Catholic chaplain and friend of our

monastery.[1] All classes: a world-known philosopher, then
a Cypriot from a fish and chips shop; all Churches, Right
Reverends, rockers, Teddy boys, musicians, mathemati-
cians, doctors.... Who are we? And all stream in together
and all call me Mother ... and I can't accustom myself to
this opening in this way, i.e. being pushed from outside. It
frightens me. I am afraid to lose the inner line and with it
the direction, i.e. my very own, what I would have to
give. But how can we ourselves steer our own ways? They
get directed. I am lucky to have a king's jester in Marina![2]

November 25th, 1971 was Sister Katherine's first
Orthodox Name Day. In celebration of the day, she and I
went into Newport Pagnell to discuss the possibilities of
lithographic printing at the Lovat Press. We came home full
of enthusiasm, to tell Mother that we must start publishing.
Mother declared that we were mad, that she would have
absolutely nothing to do with it, that we could do what we
liked, and then she sufficiently relented to agree that she *might*
help in packing books, but *nothing* else. I might as well men-
tion here that as it happened she turned out the only really
reliable proof-reader of the three of us, and also mastered the
process of 'pasting up' to save expense. But, to the end, she
insisted on the madness and that it was none of her doing.

She was of course very proud of our temerity and quietly
pushed us into every new step, particularly in what we called
our 'missionary journeys', that is, visits to bookshops, which
we dreaded above everything. We began our publishing
knowing literally nothing about either printing or publishing, starting with one card index box as a pledge to effi-
ciency: we knew nothing of copyright, nor of copies of
books received by certain libraries; we thought 'blurbs'
beneath our dignity, and retained monastic principles by having no names of authors printed on the books. It is surprising
that we condescended to titles! However, with the help of the

[1] Father Richard Catterall, then Chaplain to the Provincial House at
Clapham, Bedford, of the Daughters of The Holy Ghost. The Sisters have
remained our friends over the years, visiting and supporting us: they even
helped us to pack when we left Filgrave, in spite of their own many duties
[2] Sister Thekla's baptismal name

saints, we avoided, as far as I can see now, disgracing the good name of the Monastery and we crept out of our principled anonymity when one reviewer wrote of *The Jesus Prayer* as the work of a Benedictine monk! From December 1971, we corrected and retyped ten manuscripts for lithographing and all ten were published by October 1972. We then turned to 'real' printing with Faith Press, partly because we could not maintain the burden of faultless typing for photography, and from November 1972 to September 1974, Faith Press produced thirteen books for us, some of which were of course revised editions of the lithographed first editions, and the first pamphlet in March 1975. After that, Horne's of Whitby took over the printing of the last three pamphlets until January 1977. But this is looking ahead. In 1971, when the publishing began, we were still in Filgrave with no idea of leaving.

The publishing, of course, brought people to the Monastery, both in person and in letters. To Jo Klaver, who wrote to Mother from Holland, Mother answered on October 19th, 1972:

> We are three desert mothers now, all three longing for silence and seclusion, but it must now be found inwardly, for the demands are coming, knocking at our gate, both inward and outward, and will not be denied.... The publishing is a mad venture of faith.... We do realize that people must be helped a little at least, to a personal contact, for all have not as fine a hearing as you do.

We had constructed an outside church out of an old RAF hut in the garden, as our indoor chapel was too small for the visits of Greeks and English which now began, and Mother began to worry over the possibility of a resurgence of our old rat and mouse friends under the wooden floors. So, on November 6th, 1972 a tiny grey head peeped out of the cardboard box in which Nimrod arrived to keep the Monastery clear of vermin. He looked very small for so heavy a duty, but I hasten to add that from then until now the only mice we ever meet are those which he brings in, alive or dead. We had the best of intentions of leaving Nimmy to sleep in the garage, of never allowing him upstairs, and all the rest of the futile rules one always hopes to apply to a cat. From a very early age he took it upon himself to guard Mother, and so to the end he persisted, her head at the top of the bed, his at the bottom. When she died, he managed in a minute or two of our absence to get into her cell, and there he was, sitting erect at the bottom of the bed, completely vigilant, guarding and watching her, and only now, after nearly a year, will he sit in her chair. So Nimmy came, and the day of our grief approached when it needed all Mother's strength to keep us from despair. On January 2nd, 1973 Mother spoke to the Fellowship of St Alban and St Sergius in St Basil's House, twenty-three years after she had written her thesis in the basement, and before the end of the month, her first cancer was diagnosed and the operation followed in Northampton Hospital. Although, at the time, in view of her age and the speed of operating, the prognosis was good, she never believed that a long life would follow, and gaily took upon herself the shadow of our fear. It was soon after this first operation that Archbishop Athenagoras consecrated Mother as Abbess: as he himself said, the blessing followed the work!

In December 1973, Mother described our Filgrave Monastery to an Orthodox student in America:

You ask how we live. The monastery has two sides: one narrow, tall: on the top our three cells, below chapel (a chapel full of saints and at night one can almost see them, but no treasures, as the world sees them, in it). Beneath chapel the refectory with tables made of floorboard; white walls, brown windows and door. Annexed an old cottage-wing, low ceilings where visitors can spend a night or two. A week is for almost all of them too much solitude. The ground floor we have now to rearrange, take down a wall, etc., to make space for the Greeks and thus reduce our work. In the garden stands an RAF hut (6/12 m), made into a chapel for the 'many'. So far a made-by-us ikonostasis, to mark three entrances, with gilded rods. But I have just designed an ikonostasis and am full of awesome terror trying to find an artist for it. On the walls, paper ikons, until proper ones fall from heaven.

Then two acres spinney (oaks, ashes, larches) and a hut to run out of the world if any of us feel like it. And Sr Thekla has dug out of hard blue clay a big vegetable garden which, heavily hedged in against rabbits and pigeons, feeds us well. Sr Katherine is a bonfire genius. The books have roused many people, and the Anglicans and Roman Catholics not infrequently come to inquire. These visits are demanding. So you see, you will be welcome if you come to England again. At the moment Sr Thekla is writing a proper book on George Herbert. It will be interesting. My essay will come first, and then follows a detailed work. Sr Katherine is typing for us all the Vespers readings in English from the Septuagint. Our Services are mostly in Greek, Kathismas always in English. We have a Greek priest who comes to us once a week to celebrate a Greek Liturgy, and goes again. We are under the Ecumenical Patriarchate; surrounded by huge fields on all sides – rabbits, foxes, owls.... The printing was and is a mad venture of faith, but so mad that it somehow had to succeed. Suddenly we decided and did it. The cupboards were bursting of hidden manuscripts. There is a distinct line going from *Evil in the New Testament* (1947), the first decisive 'vision', then I thought I had to try it out first. Rewrote it as a nun in 1959 and *Sceptrum Regale* as a specific application (one could call it 'applied apophatic theology'), from there to the last two essays of *Orthodox Potential*.

Of course you may write as often as you wish and whatsoever is on your mind. There are seas still in front of you to discover and it must be exciting.

The Last Years, Normanby (1974–77)

And still, Mother was not even left to die quietly where she was. The visions of the hut, of the desert, of going physically further, away from the last security of church proximity, were still to be realized. For another year we worked quietly and steadily, but on the Feast of the Annunciation in 1974, we heard of a golf-course designed more or less on our doorstep, that we were now in the recreation belt of the new town of Milton Keynes and that it was highly unlikely that building permission would be given even for extending workrooms or cells into the garden. It was the Day of the Mother of God, who had founded our Monastery, so we could only accept her decision. And, if we were to obey, we must obey at once while Mother's strength lasted. On November 1st, 1974, with the blessing of Archbishop Athenagoras, the Monastery moved itself up the A1 to the North. It could be called our last madness and Nimmy howled dismally all the way. Yes, it could be called madness, just as Sister Katherine's leaving the security of the Abbey could be, or Mother's forgoing of academic honour, or all the other seeming nonsense at the bidding which will not be denied. We appeared to choose to leave a completed house, a reasonable climate, friends, priests, and the three of us – a dying Abbess and two elderly nuns – to betake ourselves to the bleakest strip of the coast in north-east Yorkshire, a strip so windblown that it is always three weeks behind in any harvesting, not behind the rest of England, but the rest of Yorkshire! Of course it was not our choice; we simply knew that we must go, and a month before we reached the North, Mother's secondary cancer was diagnosed.

We started life in a furnished cottage in Robin Hood's Bay, halfway down the steep bank, at the time when Mother's walking became more and more painful and the journeys for treatment to Leeds General Infirmary and Cookridge Hospital began. But by Christmas we were mercifully installed at St Bede's, on flat ground, above the Roman Catholic chapel. Without Monseigneur Lannen's charitable offer of hospitality, I do not know what we should have done. And it was here that Archbishop Athenagoras visited us and bestowed the Angelic Habit on Mother, to her deepest joy: the sign of the desert. She never wanted to be Abbess, but silently she had yearned for the Great Schema, the outward form of the inner life of prayer. It was on this visit that the Archbishop was so worried for us at the desolation of what he saw of our future monastery up on the moors in Normanby, that he suggested that we should try to stay in St Bede's! But he blessed the site, the farmhouse, and the stable which is now our chapel.

From St Bede's, Mother wrote in February 1975:

We have found a very fine plan for our monastery, perhaps
I will live to see it. It will be finished in autumn, I think.
Till then we are well lodged. Naturally my cancer is heavy
for the two others, and I would gladly go on being the soul
of the monastery, but we can have not the slightest idea
where the possibilities lie after my death; and it seems to
me if I die at such a strange point of time, it must not only
be right, but necessary; and so it is easy for me to see the
help which will come. It is fine to know that for you also
the days get brighter and lighter, and that in you there is
coming a turn, which opens, infinitely wide, and so too, in
the communication. You ask me if I would like anything. I
can now do only a very little; and sometimes I long for a
little music, perhaps a gramophone record. Whatever you
choose. We have a gramophone; but that is simply a luxury. (G).

We moved into the Monastery for Christmas 1975. It was
the same story over again. Icily cold, in spite of some heating
and electricity; no doors, some windows, but no mice and
this time the three of us together, and Nimmy. And we were
inwardly fully at peace. We knew this to be our final destination: the hut on the hill of Mother's vision, Sister Katherine's
uncharted sea, and my grey steppes.

All that we knew of Mother – the light and radiant joy in
grief, the open selflessness and tender concern, and the
unceasing living in the transcendent in the concentration of
the prayer of the heart – in these last years took on the sharpest outlines, so that the memory could not fail. Whatever
we were doing, the central point was Mother's cell, where
she sat or lay, sometimes reading, sometimes writing,
serenely ready to answer every demand on her last strength.
She suffered hours of pain before the coming of a loved visitor, so that she could take the pain-killing tablets just before
the arrival, and appear well and strong. She could trick anyone, but not us. And sometimes it was too much, and sitting
beside her I would weep, and she would say, 'It's no good,
you know, I must die and there it is.' Sometimes she was too
restless physically even to read, and then she found some rest
in music, the old violin days revived in gramophone records.

She wrote to Jo Klaver in February 1975:

> I find it good, how naturally the soul adjusts to the long
> journey, and in a way, how happily, although it seems a
> funny time to die, just at the outset of a new foundation.
> But heavenly thoughts are not earthly thoughts, and this is
> a supreme joy.

And in the same month to Paul Stanjer, former manager of
Robinson & Watkin, and most helpful over the books:

> There are now days of much joy and radiance; and there
> are very quiet days when I hold my breath. I am not suffer-
> ing much, but I am living now very consciously towards
> the End and Beginning – at last the beginning finally and
> not 'begin and begin again' – and I am happy that I can do
> this while my body is still able to carry the work. I am
> always in advance inwardly. The time is taking on other
> measures. A year seems now a long time! . . . I do some-
> times long for music. I played the violin for very many
> years. Now all goes into stillness.

At this point Jo Klaver asked her for a photograph and in
March 1975 Mother wrote with quiet amusement in reply:

> I should long ago have sent you one if I had a good one, or
> at least one which conveys some reality of myself. It seems
> impossible to achieve it! I have a very long nose, dark blue
> eyes (originally, now sometimes grey), black hair (now
> grey). I am getting quite short and fairly round; cortisone
> helping to that. In temperament I am fairly quiet, but mis-
> chievous and I love wild things. So my dearest texts in the
> Prophets were the wildest lamentations. I have a great
> sense of humour – not cynical – and would transfigure any
> criminal into a saint – and to the amusement of friends
> often did, but yet never so that I did not, at the same time,
> see the evil. I, seeing, refuse consistently to give it reality. I
> find it easy to love and nothing can stay me. And nothing
> interests me more. I am only lost with people who deny
> my mind. Then I behave like – not a fool – but an idiot,

helpless and clumsy, especially when the denial comes for the sake of the faith. Faith as against Reason (with a capital R). Now we three made an effort of finding some likenesses, best representing; but you will have to insert a twinkle into the eyes, and a brightness. So, words convey me better, I think.

It now seems relevant to insert extracts from letters Mother wrote in these last months, directly concerning herself, some to strangers and some to friends.

May 10th, 1975
I keep on saying that the way will open in clarity at my death but cannot open before. Why I say these things, I don't know. How can I know? Whether it will be light or darkness? The journeys to Leeds bring every time a step forward. But it is a bit like the Jesus Prayer, the cancer itself gently teaches one and turns one round to where it is going; with no violence, but as it were from inside.

May 24th, 1975
It is so strange to walk so straight into death and have such an immensity of unknown things in front. It already feels more and more as if this life were past and the new not yet begun. Nothing fits any more quite. But it gets easier to love people – and in a way to love anyone. . . . I all the time wonder whether one shall be frightened or not in the end. Perhaps it is natural.

June 6th, 1975
I have very short times a day when I can work and in the past weeks I tried to catch up with the sewing, to leave the other two a few habits, when I become wholly incapable ... then there comes a flop and a whole day I can do nothing at all but lie still in my bed and think, or sleep, not even read . . . sometimes I do now play a gramophone record at night . . . I love especially Schubert's String Quintet in C Major[1] which a friend sent me. He wrote it a few weeks before he

[1] cf. VIII, April 6th, 1975 (p. 112)

died, unresolved in two melodies, but ever and ever resolving into harmony.... So the time of my partial invalidity
has now set in for good. The blood count is not in order, and
the whole skeleton brittle, from thence the weariness and
pains all over at the least exertion. But I am wholly at peace
... the practical worries are now slowly resolving ... the
plan for the conversion of the farmhouse has been passed on
Wednesday, and that for an extension is being passed in
theory.... I was brought up in a very pietistic Methodist
family: no theatre, no dancing, though a lot of fun, but I
never caught up with my desire for dancing!! In heaven they
have to teach me first to dance – I shall demand it or any
equivalent.

July 18th, 1975
On the whole we are a house of mourning full of fun and Sr
Th's daily prayer is: that to the end she will be given the
strength to clown for me! I am in and out of Cookridge on an
injection course, one week hospital, four weeks out ... the
last thing they can do. I am in *much* discomfort of body – not
spirit. I am much weaker, but I can still walk in the house,
hardly outside. I can do little and I am very straightly living
towards death; but I am not yet looking very differently. My
body seems to reject every treatment form.

September 18th, 1975
Yesterday I got the message of the death of one of my own
sisters[1] – in her sleep.
   It is strange how every death brings one straight up into
another dimension of freedom, youth and new beginning,
and a wholly unknown-to-us existence, yet so deeply longed
for and as it were deeply, though not explicitly, 'known'.
And after a short while, I shall be there too; and am constantly living towards it; clearly and attentively.

October 12th, 1975
I almost overturned Father K. by saying – how it came out, I
don't know – 'if I die it means that the monastery will live.'

---

[1] Martha Gysi

October 12th, 1975

I am still fully alive in my mind and heart and I take this conscious walking towards death as a grace, and a journey which is appointed to be taken carefully and joyfully. I believe that I shall see the Monastery and live in it for a bit.

November 19th, 1975

At the moment the weather is very wild; a black, wild, beautiful sea, sun, rain, gale and sleet altogether! Sr Th. and K. are in London for three days trotting along bookshops – the terror of once a year, and my own sister from Switzerland is looking after me! So we are both sewing veils for the others as hard as we can, to leave them a supply! You did not at all weary me and need not give it another thought. I always recover and am glad to be 'called up'. We are very much concerned for both of you and would be happy to hear how you are faring. Next week will again be my hospital week – but at the moment I am reasonably well; quite quietly directed to the heavenly Jerusalem, whatever may yet come on the journey.

Christmas 1975

Sister Thekla asked me to write down the outward course of my life; but I find that more than uninteresting. It seems centuries past and I am so wholly directed forward that I cannot reach back any more.

March 21st, 1976

... the books are on the way. I am happy that some light can come out of them. As to myself, there is quite enough wading through anguish – over the building – and heaviness which probably comes from the treatment, so that I can seldom write or do anything. But it is going forward and I find it ever an immense consolation that there is a defined and unalterable day, hour, minute of the passage to the other side.

May 16th, 1976

We had a very forceful Holy Week,[1] without a priest, of course – but with all the Gospel readings (the whole Gospels)

---

[1] cf. IV, After Easter 1976 (p. 54)

and altogether nothing left out. We put a bed into Chapel for me, so it was easy, and on Good Friday night I had my watch at the Tomb, as always, and went so blissfully and peacefully to sleep, as if I were already in heaven. All that was so familiar – so near to me, as I ever and ever think of death, but Easter night was like a big, enormously big 'work', at which we all three broke down, but still battled through floods of tears. I never experienced Easter as a terrible event. But it was so far, far beyond any capacity of ours, so wholly outside our realm, and 'crushing the gates of hell' took on the meaning of crushing all that is not divine inside ourselves as well – 'the last Judgement' – and the final impossibility of judging on our part – for which our monastery from the beginning ever stood. We put four daffodil buds – the only ones we had – round the Ikon – and behold, in the damp of the still-wet walls they opened and remained fresh lying there for nine days! It was in more than one respect rather frightening; though the walls are all injected against damp! The central heating, when at last it comes, will help.

August 30th, 1976
Today was a down day, and I am so wondering – but I am going to Matins – and love it, a change of beds at 7, but I am weak and the cancer is winning, the leaving and leaving and leaving all is in every minute's thought; and bravely only to look ahead and follow whatever befalls. I see the martyrs marching in their non-sensical death which yet bore *all* sense that is in the world. It is easier to believe for others than for oneself. The northern nights are falling and often it is cold. I will – and it needs a little effort – firmly believe in the guidance of heaven through every darkness and fear. I am just unalterably now expecting the final solution and the beginning, but I see nothing except the only sense in loving – foolishly.

January 6th, 1977
You ask about Fr Lev.... When I was twenty-four, a nurse at that time, I went to Paris to stay in the house of a Russian Mother Maria, who had a home – very poor – for tramps and the destitute, and had turned a garage into a chapel. She had

been a revolutionary in St Petersburg, and in Paris she devoted her life to help the poor. She was also a friend of philosophers and writers and her house was an interesting centre. I came to help her and to become Orthodox. I had already learned Russian. There I met Fr Lev; and I saw that he understood me, and he received me very soon into the Orthodox Church on a Monday morning during the Liturgy, 1937. From then on he was my spiritual father, whom I loved and revered, and so did all my family. It was a gloriously happy time. Every Liturgy was a feast for me and quite new horizons opened up before me of a *life*, an attitude of faith far different from what I had ever known; moved, full of beauty, which wrapped up all my being, and I was well sheltered in Fr Lev's solicitude, he who flung open for me every aspect of our Church, and who was never exclusive or narrow. He was immensely learned, but only the few were allowed to know that. I then already was sometimes thinking of the monastic life, but I waited another thirteen years, during which I studied theology and philosophy, to be quite sure that I understood my faith which I loved so dearly in my heart.

April 1st, 1977

I think so much of dying, puzzling about it. I find *ekousion* and *ekon* which comes so often and strongly (in the liturgical texts) almost terrifying because it swallowed up my terror of going away so far, not of *my* will but yet of free will. This frightened me ever since – and I cannot get it out of my head. What it means to me. It is a new work every single day. I have a longing to be with people! I always loved them and I would never have thought that I could get into an enclosure; let alone our isolation – which at least is inwardly open.

May 1st, 1977

The sun shines brightly at 4 a.m. when worries awake me and then it hides again, when I grow quieter. Always this strangely anguished – over material things – waking up; every morning. It is like a ridiculous sort of passion which tears me limb from limb in the morning. Then gradually I grow calm and reasonable, I mean the grotesque fear leaves me and the grip lets go its grasp. And all this about what I shall soon leave for good – it is strange.

June 1st, 1977 [to Winifred Frohne who sent money to us from America for a church bell, from herself and her students]
We love our bell. I am very deeply touched at the loving remembrance and the dear gifts, from each one, and the Vietnamese. I can hardly believe it, how you have made us so alive and present to them.

After a very cold winter, we have now summer days. I am alone this afternoon and it is very still. It could be anywhere in the world.

September 2nd, 1977
... it gives us hope that they will look after the Monastery in heaven.... I definitely went down these last weeks and the last chemotherapy left me with one side of my face down – I look like nothing on earth – one eye half shut, and a lot of pain in hip and head, behind the ears – and we all had 'flu and a lot of guests – three Americans – a priest and his wife – so we had a lovely Assumption Liturgy. I have still my spirit all one, but I must take stuff for pain more often. It looks as if the near-end were coming nearer. I am still up a bit – I can't eat tidily because one end of the mouth does not shut. So we take that as fun; and in two weeks a publisher[1] comes to talk about I don't know what. He knew me before.... I am very peaceful and happy and curious what the other side will be like, and much less worried now.... Sr Thekla got it through now that we shall have our own little graveyard in our fields, and that gives her all the strength!! Hospital next week (8.9). We do it on two days[2] but from the journey I broke two ribs ... three weeks in bed ... still I am not wasting away ... the tomatoes are just turning red in the greenhouse and the wheat harvest will soon come ... there

[1] John Todd
[2] this was only made possible by the hospitality and tender care shown to us by Clare Spencer in Leeds: when she was away, Tom and Mollie Catterall showed us equal kindness

is a sense of life here.... I had a letter from someone who was excited over *The Hidden Treasure*, as 'coming home' and introduced himself so.

End of September, 1977
Your Priory will be so full of life and bustlery, how I wish I could look in, but I do that always. Perhaps it will all be exciting. I catch myself thinking, 'Oh, I'll tell them later' or 'I'll find Sr Thekla a proper printing machine later';[1] quite mad, but what am I to do with you lot? Let's be merry and without tears.

November 1st, 1977
My eyes; one has a slightly paralyzed muscle and the other is weakened. Together it is a circus. And I was much giddy – as if I had had a bit of another stroke. I lie in bed, can do nothing, I hardly see now and the days are long. Sometimes I have raging headaches, not every day. All this would be frightening if I let it but I want to run merrily – whatever my silly head chooses to do. And I often think of the light coming – nearer and growing bigger and bigger. The doctor thought of warning me that I have still a quite considerable time ahead of me, but that is in God's hands alone. This week certainly I was very ill and often I am so nervous – physically this is the worst chemotherapy torture. I am hungry for food for the mind – but unable to read – so I cannot even sort the candles because of being giddy so soon, even when I talked today for half an hour. So I say good night. Write to me. Do not be too much sad. I am all the time thinking and wondering and believing in a solution as yet unseen.

November 3rd, 1977
It is possible that I have had one or two little strokes with facial paralysis, now symmetrical again, but with noises in the ears; the hearing in one ear is very weak and I get bad headaches on the other side. The eye on this side has been

[1] within three months of her death, a totally unexpected gift of money enabled us to buy a 'new' second-hand printing press

slightly paralysed, so I see double and have to close one eye; also I seem to have lost my balance a little – all this in the last two or three months. I can still think, and am generally happy and contented. All that can either mean cancer in the brain or the result of the chemotherapy. I often feel sick as well – perhaps the worst of the lot.

So we crawl on all fours heavenwards, and yet at the same time we run speedily and youthfully round all the corners without making a song about it. (G).

On November 12th, Father Kallistos, who had quietly taken on our spiritual care, travelling all the way regularly from Oxford, came urgently to anoint and give Mother her Communion. He was anyway due to come on the 27th for a Liturgy but it was felt better not to wait. On Friday morning at twenty-past nine – November 25th, 1977 – our Mother, the Abbess Maria, died. We had been with her day and night since the Wednesday, but when she died we could hardly be sure, the movement was so imperceptible. She was buried in our church burial ground on the 27th, and the Liturgy was celebrated, but instead of singing she lay in the middle of the church, a smile of serenity on her face; the journey of sixty-five years had reached its loved destination.

Our Monastery stands, farmhouse, stable-church and the new wing. Here Mother lived, amidst the fields and distant white-horsed sea, for nearly three years. She would look over at the Abbey ruins in Whitby, delighted that St Hilda had also built where it might seem impossible. And Mother lies now in our own blessed earth, her little iron cross looking up at the tall iron cross which surmounts the burial ground. On her grave flowers grow, and the wheat sways golden a few feet away. The wind sweeps across with its North Sea gusts. In those last few days of her life, when she could no longer speak to us, we saw her hurrying towards a loved meeting. She knew that her work would begin after death, and we saw the concentration of her whole being to the point of the End. Dying, she had such a smile of joy, as we had never seen in life. She had arrived in the longed-for land. But we? We have been left to live these last years alone, and to work. Now again two, but Mother pleading for us in heaven.

Who, then, was our Mother? She was to the uttermost
austere, frankly ignoring all sentimentality, bad thinking,
and self-excusing; she could pierce to the lie inside self-pity,
whatever its disguise. She never condemned spiritual false-
ness, she would merely remark that she found it all boring.
She paid no honour to the devil for her sickness, her pain, the
tribulations, threats and cruelty through which her monastery had survived, or her own agonies of heart. She took it all
upon herself, with never a thought of regret or reproach. To
live with Mother was to live with total integrity on every
level, and to suffer love is more painful than to suffer
reproach or rebuke. With the inner austerity came the outer
fun, and the hiding of herself unless she knew that she would
be understood. And she never gave answers. But, above all,
in her was the fragrance of innocence: the ever-flowing
source of transfiguring love. So, this can be nothing but a
book of comfort, for she wrote as she lived, and her letters
bring this comfort of love: of the storm-wind of silence in the
whisper of the Spirit.

I THE COMMUNION OF SAINTS

Mother of God – saints – martyrs – ubiquity

The saints are real, and their presence on earth, inside the Mystery of Christ, remains an objective reality. The Mother of God, on earth and in heaven, is close and familiar but ever beyond our comprehension unless she, herself, gives a direct command. The Mother of God and the saints are our friends and will help us, if we do not interfere too much ourselves; so on earth we need never be alone, and, in them, we are promised a personal heaven. And, in them, we see the true measure of success which alone is our comfort in the work of love.

It was her love for the saints, in heaven and on earth, which made Mother Maria reticent over 'ecumenical' efforts of 'fellowship' and anything which, for her, could be seen as *im*personal love. Her friends were ever across the Churches, but as *persons*, not representatives, *within* the Communion of Saints. And once they walked into her life – Protestant, Anglican, Roman Catholic, or her own Orthodox, priest, monk, nun, or any man, woman, or child – they never walked out of her heart.

———————————

[*No date*] *1952*
If there were no Communion of the Saints, then could there be no heaven for creatures. It means that there will be *pure* vision, yet personal and everyone his very own, and altogether the whole – that it is which guarantees our *personal* existence in heaven. Otherwise we would plunge into God and disappear.

1

[No date] 1952
One cannot think enough of the martyrs – who sum up the
task of love by the bare suffering of death. There is such
graceful and bare poverty in it – nothing achieved, visibly –
nothing but being the object of violence; and empty hands,
except for love; and we cannot even be sure that we are
consciously bearing love at the hour of death. Heavenly zeal
is *repose in God*; profound inner rest; and repose redeems
earth's suffering; we need love for the world, and respect for
its suffering.

May 14th, 1954
Courage consists only in looking beyond, and in the strong
sense of the presence of God and of his saints.

July 1955
My vision of God is the vision of his love in the Communion
of Saints.

April 18th, 1958 (G)
But I have the true and real deep joy of the Church, it came
when I discovered the saints; the Church in heaven; which
surrounds us and carries us and lives with us. Since that time
the Church is my home, in which I can 'dance and sing', but
also weep if I want to weep; so I can never more fall out of the
world; and you should know that there are friends there to
learn to know; but of course everyone must find his own and
in his own way.

December 21st, 1958 (G)
For a soul, which wants to live only for itself, the *Communio
Sanctorum* can only mean a nameless pain, because life consists in being open to all people, the love for God gets active
in the love for people. God is also in hell and to find him there
is wonderful.

December 25th, 1961 (G)
I am ever again amazed how the first Christians, in persecution, kept so finely the 'proportions'; and how everything
found the right place by itself, including the persecuting

State. A long time ago we were given an old ikon, which depicts St Dimitri of Salonica in martyrdom. How does the Church depict his martyrdom? The young martyr, high up on a steed, with flying cloak (which represents the Holy Spirit) and a long spear; under the horse, small and dwarfish – a dwarf – the persecuting Caesar Diocletian crouches on his dwarfish white horse, which also crouches to the ground, and the spear pierces the Caesar's ear, to open it to other values. This is the first theme, which is later changed to the battle with the dragon. But the dragon is also the persecuting State and the victory *is* the martyrdom itself. In the bigness and the dwarfishness is suggested that in the martyrdom evil is overcome, though on another level. It is not a contest between two powers, which either one or the other can win, as it is often depicted today.

August 1965
I am the first to accept loneliness as far as it is livable; but I am also the first to rejoice in the Communion of Saints on earth. And this consists in love which respects the suffering of the *other*, and sees the glory in it, and does not try to fight it or take it away, because it would mean taking the ultimate glory away. To see one's own suffering as glory is impossible, but it is *very easy* to see the other person's suffering as glory; and this is the transfiguring strength of love. The question as to whether the suffering is mental or physical is of almost no account; and whether it is innocent or not is also not so important. But what God makes of it is important. All by himself he builds up a fortress of strength for others out of years of bleak, barren loneliness.

June 22nd, 1967
'God alone' can never mean anything wider and deeper than the total acceptance of his will and the total orientation towards the final cause, and no determining power given to penultimate immanent causes. This is costly, but to put 'God alone' against men and fellow combatants is to deny the *Communio Sanctorum* and to fall out of the church and the gospel teaching of the closest communion in all things, in every battle, in every joy. See St Paul, did he ever make any

such remarks? Instead, he never wearied of stressing his
deepest concern and inner preoccupation for his children.
Anxieties, innermost presence with them at every moment.
He would have taken it for a denial of the Holy Spirit, if it
were otherwise. And St John identified the love of God and
man and made them presuppose one another. It just will not
hold water; and my vocation has always been the revelation
of the Communion of Saints. To deny this, even in the smallest degree, is to darken one's own vision of God and that
direct, immediate grasp on his immediate presence and solicitude.

July 12th, 1967
. . . or of Christ's prerogative being impaired by the veneration of saints, which is measuring by a finite and poor standard of love.[1]

May 14th, 1968 [written in reply to an Anglican monastic
discussion on liturgical reform][2]
I find the Presence theme very far-reaching and clear. It is so
clear what the Reserved Sacrament replaced: the presence of
the ikons. The Communion of Saints converged on the Blessed Sacrament. The presence of the heavenly Church: the
Orthodox are brought up with it so carefully that not a step is
unguarded, unlinked, from the immediate *context* of the life
on the other side; and also giving the sense of the presence of
the saints as they are *now*, the person remaining inside the
transfiguration into Christ; history and transfigured history;
history inside the 'operation of the End'. If now ikons and
Reserved Sacrament are both abandoned, it will be 'remembrance' taking the place of 'Presence' more and more. And
then at once comes the claim of the individual experience of
meeting Christ (claimed also in Bultmann theology). When
the Presence vanishes on the objective level, it must be found
again somewhere, and there opens up all the grace and pitfalls
of the 'personal experience', which can no longer be shared so
easily since it is more closely linked with unsharable sense-
experience: less transcendent, less universal and less peaceful

[1] cf. VI, April 17th, 1976 (p. 83)
[2] cf. III, April 16th, 1968 (p. 25) and III, Eastertide 1968 (p. 26)

in itself, though the actual experience may be the experience of peace.

November 5th, 1968
It is my everlasting boast that the Abbey[1] has never sunk to propaganda, and that is her strength; as if one had to help God and the saints all the time! They are far more imaginative and skilled in finding ways than we are; but they don't like it if one 'helps' them too much, somehow. They very quickly, and certainly with humour, say: 'All right, then, do it on your own'; and I think, of all things, I would not fear any moment more than hearing this. It would seem to me like a death sentence from heaven. Hooker had a lovely expression: if God finds some 'tractable ones', he makes them profit by suffering and persecution and isolation.

December 2nd, 1968
There is one English hymn I always say when I feel too anguished; and today we sang it full force in Chapel – 'For all the saints who from their labours rest' – though I occasionally think they might help one a little better. I wonder how it is the other side; and what they think at our grumblings – of course they laugh – nicely, though. But really, we always feel the house full of them, one almost meets them; so we never feel to be only two, but rather the house full to bursting.

November 17th, 1969
... and listen to the music of the saints and light *all* the candles – the Chapel must feast this week – that I can *feel* its feasting life and death.

June 4th, 1972 [to a Roman Catholic monk]
We with our happy Orthodox 'muddles' on the top level, do not so carefully distinguish between heaven and earth; and happily claim the presence of the heavenly hosts and all the saints *in person*, for wherever we are, because they *must* look after us.[2] So, perhaps, one day you will find your Abbey and

[1] St Mary's Abbey, West Malling
[2] cf. vii, December 29th, 1974 (p. 92)

hermitage thronged with Orthodox monks; and they will tell you all the secrets of the desert; – and of heaven.

March 2nd, 1975
Once I had a sort of real vision of the Mother of God – only once – when I least expected it, and it said in my heart, 'It is all quite different,' with a lovely smile at our earthly ideas of her. What surprises we shall have of what made sense and what did not.

Christmas 1975
Perhaps one could find strength in the minute minority of the martyr-company, and not ask for more. I come to it more and more explicitly.

March 25th, 1976
The Liturgical anniversary of Filgrave's death-sentence; and the beginning of struggles. Last night I woke up at 2 a.m. and could not go to sleep any more. The unbearable pressure had lifted. The room seemed filled with an unutterable peace, and the immediate presence of the Mother of God, who two years ago had told me: 'I am going, you can stay if you like.' And this night it was as if she told me firmly that she had taken over; chapel and all ... but also the pressing here in hospital that I should make an inward turning to life again till I am definitely called to the other side. They actually reckon with a prolongation, as no other serious symptoms so far have appeared, and for the first time, I feel this as a definite calling to reorientate back to life; and to leave all in the hands of the Mother of God, to whom our Monastery has always belonged. Today, weary of the night, I quietly stayed in bed pondering where the reality lies. Moments of peace always seem the truth of our position, and terror the prison of lies, where I literally often feel stifled like a person with no air, in a coffin, and of late so inwardly paralyzed, that I could not move. Perhaps it just means that I must now be courageous, and within the reduction, be joyful and trusting.... It all seemed so definite, precise and clear-cut, like a call in the night; and the end of the transition and the beginning of the new.

June 23rd, 1977 [concerning a wish to write about the life of the Mother of God]
I should be very careful about the Mother of God. There is a very great Mystery in the way she lived hiddenly for so many years; and it would need a very direct command from herself to write about what you *cannot* know. I so feel what people in our age need so much more than anything else, and what the Orthodox Church has so faithfully preserved, is the knowledge that there is one great divine Mystery – the presence of Christ in the world – and many Mysteries inside that great Mystery, which we can and may adore, and contemplate with our heart and mind, but which we shall never comprehend, because our faculties are too small. And here precisely lies the source of our joy. We have something to look forward to, when we shall see face to face. I think the transference of the faith is a delicate thing which is never in our own hands, and that it is safer to limit ourselves to the things which are given into our reach and possible knowledge.

II THE MIND

Bad and good thinking – doubt – philosophy
lived – limitation of reason – consent of the mind

As long as we are alive in this world, it is impossible for us not to think, and nonsense to deny the mind, as the denial is already an act of thinking. Such non-acknowledgement of the mind can only result in *bad thinking*. Good thinking is reason within Reason. The mind is moved to thinking by all the assaults of doubt, in every direction, for God gives us no absolute knowledge. Thus, philosophy is not a theory but a life to be lived, in the reasonable resolution of doubt, that is of the practical problem. Philosophy is no more an ideology than faith. Both must be lived within the context of the world. In Platonism we find the way of philosophy lived and, thus, its kinship to the attitude of the Orthodox faith: the working on the hypothesis, ever prepared to begin again, as we do in repentance: the humility of mind which knows what it cannot comprehend and will not attempt to peer into the mind of God: the glad recognition of the limitation of our thought which leads to the consent of the mind to the faith: that is the surest foundation to faith for it cannot be disillusioned. The Platonic way is a lonely one, and unexciting, for it seeks no success, it will not give the answer, nor entertain in speculation. But it is the way which lays the foundation for dying to the world, and the way which acknowledges that, whatever we do, we are only partial. How could we live as monks, or as philosophers, if others did not fight?

[No date] 1952
There are mothers who, with a beast's instinct, find out how to deprive their child of the essentials; and what the child needs; and for no other reason but to try to imprint their own smallness on the child's soul. There are so few humble parents who know that they have God in their child and something *more* than themselves.

July 1955
There is so much lack of the essential humility of the mind, which brings such a great freedom and opens the wings. Our time needs nothing more urgently than minds who bring those things together which others have pulled to pieces. The Christians have the secret, if only they would use it.

May 1956
A vision of the mind demands patience and fortitude, incomprehension belongs integrally to it. It demands a patience and fortitude far beyond that demanded of any vision of the heart. And it remains always in the 'beggar's cloak' because it surpasses normal faculties. To have the privilege of seeing beyond necessitates the having poverty of earth in every sense – otherwise it is not real. Philosophers, even those with the smaller visions, are *always* lonely and homeless. The main thing is not to let the other feel the gap.

December 17th, 1959 (G)
... the older I get, the more I become conscious that the form and shape of an intellectual content has yet a much higher significance and a higher 'dignity' than I had thought earlier in my impatience to find and to understand the content. Our life here[1] seeks also the most beautiful form for the highest content, while the form of our way of living allows the content to grow almost unnoticed, if we do not cheat. I see an effect on both sides, that the beautiful form lets the content ripen, and the content creates and determines the form, in our imperfect world; but in the perfect, form and content are a unity and something final, because where the

[1] Benedictine Rule

form represents perfectly a content, there can be only *one* form, but in our world there are many forms for every content, because a perfect representation can never be reached.

October 10th, 1960
I have once followed up the question why God has given us the Bible in such a frail form[1] – the beggar's cloak; and I answer that God in his goodness gave us his word in a form which does not exclude doubt. Then I see what doubt means, and come to the conclusion that our process of thinking necessarily, by nature, must work itself through doubt in very many ways. When, then, God did not exclude doubt for us, it means that he gave us the Bible in a form which we can integrate into our *life*, which is adapted and adequate to our process of life and thought; so that we can actually live in the Bible and the Bible in us. Then I see what it would mean if God had thrown his word at us in the form of absolute truth with a shattering evidence. We should perish under it, simply because it would be something totally alien to us. We could do nothing with it, it would in all eternity arrest our process of thought, and cause us to die a sort of second death. This I develop all very carefully and in the joyful conviction that God has given us the best in the best way, when he visited us in 'the beggar's cloak'.

[No date] 1961
Non-thinking only begins *beyond* thought.

August 1965
The philosophers are those who suffer most keenly the limitations of reason, because they use it most; and I will go further, they are those who rejoice most keenly in the possibility of getting beyond, *not* in speculation but in love active and lived.

March 25th, 1967
I am myself reduced to the core, but I see in that irreducible Platonist core an invincible *réduit*, and to live in it, in bare

---

[1] *The Hidden Treasure*

austerity, refusing all the trappings of seeing faith, of faith forcing itself into more – or rather less – than faith, the one really and deeply satisfying and safe position; but also the chief work of Christian Platonism: that one *can* live when the relativity of every expression of faith and one's own knowledge is accepted; to every form of a true critical mind given free scope, because nothing can be lost. I am reliving and rethinking it constantly, now in the joy and privilege of opening this way to my one novice.... The core is the joyful destruction of the double ignorance in every sphere of life, thought, faith. I mean that very far-reaching, almost to the full extent, of the not-knowing of Socrates and I find it a great and strong joy.

June 20th, 1967
I think a lot of Gauss; where I knew what Platonism costs at the worldly forefront; and I think of the last few months of utter darkness; and I feel these months to be the ultimate 'work'. All the prophets thought they *were* alone; and so do perhaps all real philosophers. *Why* is Bultmann so attractive to the young minds? *What* is so satisfactory for them?

June 22nd, 1967
Platonism is ultimately the *attitude* (not a system), not to be *willing* to accept anything, evil or not, from the hands of the devil, but only from the hands of God directly, i.e. with the ultimate trust that they have in them the possibility of transfiguration and transformation.

To see the OT attitude in this light in a thousand reflections. God sending all the most appalling evils and then being distraught that they do not bring men back to him.

That Christian Platonism is so satisfying because it demands no transfiguration or adaptation or self-defence. It is applicable in any situation, conquering the world.

Ultimately it ends in the humility of the mind as the key to the overcoming of evil and protection against mental disorder.

June 29th, 1967
Another part is the renunciation of assertions about the Mind

of God (ideas as the Mind of God). In the end far more certainty comes out, and an invincibility, in thought, against doubt, on all levels. *But*, one must renounce, and after all, what infinite misery would it be if we had to expect nothing more the other side than the archetypes of this world,[1] i.e. this life a little cleansed out, *in* its logical content. I want an entirely different life, with different minds and means of apprehension, a world of surprises, and this we are told it will be.

August 2nd, 1967
But in the end I think we shall win. It is so difficult to pass on Platonism, because it is really a way of life, an attitude of thought, a total renunciation of presumption; and this can be better passed on by living.... In all the wildness a shape emerges; if we are left to our own judgement. If not, all the strength, still left, will just be consumed by futile battle. Stupidity is a sin, *the* sin, *the* capital, 'mortal' sin.

[The following extracts between October 10th, 1967 and May 25th, 1970 are all taken from letters written to Sister Katherine when we were in Filgrave and she was still at St Mary's Abbey.]

October 10th, 1967
The remaining in the not-seeing, as the ultimate grace and joy of our earthly existence, is the Platonic endurance of the limitation of our mind which our heart can transcend by love.... We were thinking where the hitch was wherein the Neo-Platonists did not keep to Plato's self-limitation in the assertion of *Nous* being the Mind of God, and all the confusion which follows on that; and how difficult it is to maintain the reserve, because discussions must cease at the 'not-knowing', and people really far more want the fun of discussion than the austerity of truth.

November 17th, 1967
I was thinking of the impasse of 'election' – against the

---

[1] cf. IX, June 20th, 1967 (p. 120)

Platonic view of starting with love in which no doubt has room and therefore no assurance is needed. Election is a hypothesis. It is a *human* way of defining the fact that some believe; and also a reasonable explanation of man's belonging or not to God, in the attempt to explain a Mystery which is one's life (and as little as we can get behind our reason and look at it, so can we behind our life), i.e. the whole question rests upon the refusal of acknowledging the limitation of our reason and thinking.

The Platonist's refusal to peep into God's action, and refusing to acquiesce in the utter impasse of a false question and the arbitrary finite solution to infinity – those, who were accused of being rationalists – struck the death-blow to the rationalism of the Reformation by starting from the other end; not by thinking, but by doing, whereby our *consent* is a pre-eminent *act* which engages us wholly and forever.

August 29th, 1968
What is once seen by reason as well as by the heart is inescapable in its demand upon the whole person. I read again in an Orthodox article about Christianity being *anti*-logical. It is a heresy which wrenches the human person to bits and leads into Nothing. Then the creation *was* a failure. But how and what they think logic is! It is a dreary world of conflict. I always feel a sort of inner 'flop' when I read anything like it.

October 22nd, 1968
I relive again the young excitement when I wrote it twenty-one and a half years ago,[1] and when in one fell swoop *understood*, and never not understood. The Gospel had opened from inside to my mind as well as my will, and had swallowed me up.

November 12th, 1968
I think the chief thing is to learn to think hypothetically: starting from the assumption that *every* expression is necessarily inexact; and every geography of concepts, or 'field of apprehension', is merely one way of apprehension. Then one

[1] *Evil in the New Testament*, in its first form in 1947

has to dive wholly into the thinker's field – to view it from within the context of *his* thought. Otherwise one will never get at what he really meant. And one must use the steps he takes delicately; I mean, so that they are never like solid stones, but can move, and in different contexts modify their sense. It is like working with ideas as principles of research, but never ultimately stopping at a conclusion which makes sense, for it will lead further. This is also part of the humility of the intellect: not to stop, but to be ready to go on, and partly modify what is gained and never to 'sit on it'.[1]

November 19th, 1968
I am quite lost with the new-age theology, in the sense that I perfectly understand it, but what I don't understand is that they like it like that or find it in any way interesting. But it is perhaps a flat passage which one day will again lead upwards.

January 29th, 1969
It [philosophy] is and remains for me *medicina mentis*. This fine and healthy 'distance' in thought – the transcendence of the 'cares of this world' and the glad submission of the spirit. Also the beatitude of that land beyond individual tangles and moans of the body – the heavy horsecart which so often screeches and will no longer play quite fairly.

February 25th, 1969
The choice for anyone is never philosophy or not, but good or bad philosophy, underlying life and action. To leave the world to a course of superficial *thinking* means to leave it to its most formidable danger, because it then has no means with which to encounter the onslaught of ideologies.

April 30th, 1969
They [the young] have lost all capacity for seeing within the lostness which underlies faith. Faith without this underlying lostness is no faith. And asserted lostness is a form of assertion which faith has renounced. It is the flight before doubt, and the doubt has become part of the terror of war and threat

---

[1] cf. VIII, August 22nd, 1973 (p. 104)

from all sides, as if these had invaded their souls and were now experienced as doubt. But the source is fear; not thought leading to doubt. And one can well understand that they 'march' and must shout and *do* something to banish the paralysis of fear. It is this that makes the barrier.

May 6th, 1969
... the bare, austere purity of seeking Truth ... the transparent water with 'nothing between': it is this which feeds the soul so potently, with the severe austerity of non-assertion.

May 20th, 1969
People want to play and be interesting. What thought means they are not interested in, because it bears a weight of obligation and demand and the dying to self; and the making of thought the means for self-set purposes – then Truth goes further and further and they are left to their own game.

May 28th, 1969
I found a lovely bit on reason.[1] It is unPlatonic to assume reason to be a capacity which man *has* by *nature*. Reason is the gift of the Creator to the creature, it is not a capacity as an existing fact. It is only a *potential* power which can only become effective with the *ethical* use of *all* the powers of the soul, i.e. when the whole soul is directed towards the Perfect. Reason is not an original natural talent of man, but a *higher power through which man can transcend himself* (i.e. the real use of reason is the crossing out of oneself).... And in his constant emphasis that the *question* must be right. There are questions asked that are wrong. Silly questions have silly answers – how often did I hear that!

July 24th, 1969 [In reply to a claim that abstract imagery is the most adequate medium for depicting the incomprehensible God.]
With mathematics you remain within the human reason, and this is the profoundly despairing thing about it. In humanity-image you have the suggestion of the whole per-

---

[1] Gauss lecture notes

son. In abstract image you have the imposition of what is
meant to be a more adequate representation, but the abstrac-
tion is only the human mind; there you remain imprisoned
by the intrinsic claim of adequacy, more subtle and proud,
more bursting with double ignorance than in the representation of a person, which obviously is inadequately drawn. A
bad crucifix is more suggestive than a good abstract because
there is no imprisonment involved. It is meant only to be a
hint, but an abstract is an interpretation, and therefore
imposed with a certain finality, and it does not suggest the
knowledge of its own inadequacy. Humility is the most
potent way of hinting at the divine presence. . . .

Of one of the English interpreters [of Hegel], Gauss said:
'An Englishman in fierce battle with a German monster' got
himself so involved: 'I wish he would explain his explana-
tions.' And – trust the English – when Kant and Hegel (millions of miles apart) got known in England (about 1860) they
thought they were *all the same* 'German idealism', admirably
suited to fight positivism!! and to defend the Christian faith!!

July 31st, 1969
I found a lovely passage:[1] as every solution is the outcome of
conflict and contradiction, a wide knowledge must needs
have passed through many trials and hardships, and it cannot
be expected that the philosopher will be understood or found
out. The deeper his knowledge, the less will he find understanding (as St Thérèse's sufferings: the truer, the less
shown).

August 20th, 1969
. . . that a true philosopher could not expect to be understood; to be one meant to take upon oneself the pain and
strenuous labour of thought and that every insight, having
passed through the conflict of doubt, *cannot* simply be shared
and transmitted. To share it would mean for the other to be
ready for doubt and pain, the higher the more poignant. And
we have no right to demand this of another.

---

[1] ibid.

October 17th, 1969

The digression in the second hypothesis[1] is most important – the soul moving the ideas – the precondition of our thinking. Then, I just thought now, one might see two concentric circles and *each* going every moment through the 'sudden' – that 'nought' outside time – which evades our reason, ungraspable as death and eternity. In the world of ideas – the big circle, and again in our limited reason (where no idea is unmixed with its contradictory, where only thought within contraries is possible) we have to pass through that 'sudden'. It is like the big Cross and the little crosses. The big Death and the little deaths, as the precondition of life altogether, of motion, and the life of communication, i.e. of love.

The 'sudden' in its flavour of eternity is also the 'nought', the quotient in the differential calculus, that strange passage through death *every* day ... but also generalized, the cycles becoming but an emphasized law of life; as it were, a more explicit realization of it. And in *Parmenides* it is seen in big letters. The soul (as principle of life) cannot bring motion and life except through that passage of death. With no transition, right at the heart, no longer expressible in words commonly understood, it is shown to be the law of reason; and here is the focal point of the humility of the mind: the 'sudden' being, as it were, dialectically, the eternity point *and* death. With this, re-enacted in every process of thinking, the whole late Plato unfolds.

December 5th, 1969

I found a lovely sentence in Gauss:[2] Plato does not acknowledge anything as effective except that which *works*, is working, has power to work; which is the soul alone, i.e. facts *can* not act, have no power, and in themselves, except as material to work upon for the soul, have no reality. Reality comes only from the soul but is not. Only what *works* reality is real.

December 17th, 1969

There is another thought just come to me; the breaking away

[1] *Parmenides*, 155E–157B
[2] *Philosophischer Handkommentar zu den Dialogen Platos, Dritter Teil, Erste Hälfte*, 206, note 2 (Bern, Herbert Lang, 1960)

from tradition on one side, and my refusal to repeat endlessly
what others have thought; as if no one had the right to begin
at the beginning. Everyone, in thought, *must* begin at the
beginning because thought is the whole *person*.... 'Let us
begin again' – 'Let us look at it again' – up and down, up and
down the ladder of thought. It is like the 'Again and again in
peace, let us pray to the Lord.' The patient dialectic mind that
never asserts finality nor sits on its momentary findings.
'Let's start again from the beginning' – Let's pray a thousand
times the same thing, as if we had never prayed, and it is new
every time.

January 30th, 1970
But of course the real difference lies in that Cudworth
assumes the ideas as 'entities' (but even that with caution) in
the 'Mind of God', which is an assertion that cannot be made
philosophically. I always revel in the sober limitation of its
being *hypotheses* which we must make if we wish to explain
the finite phenomena.

May 25th, 1970[1]
We could not live as Platonic philosophers – seeing the
innermost core in everything and not acting till we see – if
there were not others who do act and fight; the world would
stand still. But I see it in a very special kind of way, thinking
of Fr N. who *can* act in faith alone; we have to wait for the
inner evidence. I am very happy and feel I have at last caught
up with Gauss here. I always knew it, but never so experienced it in the full impact of truth and joy. It is the never-
ending source of humility and more and more knowledge of
our narrow limitations which is the gate to wide, wide horizons.

March 17th, 1971 [to Professor Armstrong]
Over the CPs[2] I have a growing uneasiness about the 'Divine
Mind', very much like your own, and I am cross with myself
that I was not alert enough to the problems when writing the
thesis. I can no longer accept – and I always did have a creeping feeling – any talking of the divine mind as if we knew

---

[1] cf. v, March 24th, 1976 (p. 71)   [2] Cambridge Platonists

what it did, and how it worked; and I find Plotinus' bashing and smashing almost more adequate, because it is so absurd. Yes – the gravitation, if once the rendering logical account is abandoned – towards the identification with the divine mind! It is unavoidable. But with the reticence also the archetypes fall – because they also presuppose, on our part, omniscience; and the solution 'as one whole' of 'our life as one whole', while we find solution and the meaning of our life only from problem to problem anew. The absoluteness and finality would crush us and give us no field of action. In a way, the divine *Nous*: as the totality, act plus content: one whole, immutable, etc. – would – if we could *really* think it – be the death of our mind; but with the first hypothesis[1] I did not mean the divine *mind*. I meant the 'Perfect' – beyond, which we cannot even adequately utter: the nearest must be the double negation.

August 22nd, 1973
The *consent of the mind* (Whichcote) is the acknowledgement that we cannot act on knowledge, only on hypothesis.

October 24th, 1973
'God lit a light in our hearts, towards the illumination of knowledge of his glory (or the glory of God) in the face of Christ.'[2]
A very careful sentence.
Towards – never fulfilled.
Knowledge of glory – only possible in part – by illumination,
   it is the second 'wisdom' of 1 Corinthians 1.21, etc.

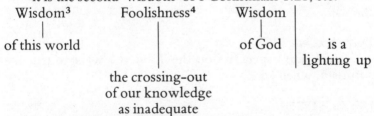

   Wisdom[3]   Foolishness[4]   Wisdom
     | | |
of this world   of God   is a
                                                  lighting up
              the crossing-out
              of our knowledge
              as inadequate
But lighting up to a knowledge – of the *mind* and heart.

[1] *Parmenides*, 137C–142A
[2] 2 Corinthians 4.6
[3] cf. The Double Crossing-out of the Dialectic, *Foreword* (p. x)
[4] cf. VIII, December 8th, 1973 (p. 106)

November 22nd, 1973
I wrote lately[1] a talk on 'the Fool', my beloved Fool at the
End-point, the Prophet-Fool, the Philosopher-Fool, the
Christian-Fool, interpreting of course the humble working of
the mind, but also crossing it out in its absolute relevance in
the face of eternity, where new measures prevail, new horizons open, and a new life begins.

December 8th, 1973
... spoke of the Jesus Prayer and found that what he calls
going out of the intellect, I call going into it. 'Intellect' must
be kept as a 'good' word, or you will get stuck. We must
work at the integration of our thinking into the faith. Love
and Truth (with a capital T) are one; and most one for us
Orthodox.

January 1974
In Image? You must imagine all the OT prophets standing,
looking beyond, seeing the solution in the present disaster:
'With love everlasting have I loved thee'; a miserable remnant
travelling the way back to the ruined City, spiritless – the
Fool. Or the philosopher-fool – his soul 'standing upon
itself', 'looking up to the ideas';[2] and never using his reason
for his own profit or comfort. He is, of course, a super-fool.
The prophet is under constraint – with his prophetic,
impetuous soul. But the philosopher could otherwise; and
chooses the 'foolery' entirely by free will; in the highest
meaning. For free it is only towards the transcendent,
unhampered by worldly motives, which, as ends, determine
the will.

December 29th, 1974
... but I don't speculate on the Trinity. I want to get my
surprises, when I die.

[No date] 1975
We are called to work within the not-knowing, yet in the

[1] cf. x, September 25th, 1973 (p. 138)
[2] *Phaedo*, 65C

incessant presence of the *causa finalis* inside the imperfect, ever inadequate, ever jealous, longing for the perfect, not wearying because of the love of that presence. And with that may come the truly dialectic way of thinking which frees the mind to work and frees the mind to prayer, to the apprehension of the unattainable glory, the Mystery. And 'unattainable' precisely is the word of urgency for working for it, where 'reverent agnosticism' is manifest in its cheap escape. And precisely on the level with fundamentalist fantasy; and its stubborn denial of truth; minds enslaved in the fear of losing the faith, or of doing the wrong thing; both escaping doubt instead of working with it.

January 4th, 1975
Where our mind and my love is not acknowledged – or, rather not seen – I am utterly lost, shaky, fearful, and not myself; and already there was that characteristic lostness in me with Fr S. which immediately alarmed Sr Th., not without cause; my Achilles heel, for which perhaps I have to die in the end; reasonably so. I begin – more and more – to *fear* mindlessness, and non-love of a loving *mind*. Humility is an attitude of *mind*. But by mind, I mean more; certainly not rationalism.

January 28th, 1975 (G)
I was a little sad that S. has given up her way. Why is it that high political aims always go now with love affairs and not from spiritual motives only? Also, I find it hard to accept that everything must be done in groups, and that people no longer seek, await and long for the courage to live a spiritual life on their own initiative. In this way, it seems to me, everything becomes so cheap. But I daresay that is totally unjust in view of the difficulties.

March 24th, 1975
Where are mind and heart so inextricably one as in our prayers? It is the wrenching apart where my realm of work lies – to heal that, and ever cry out for healing. It is there that

the world perishes; at the denial of the mind as one with the
heart by the Christians who should bind them together – and
now the Orthodox also in full cry against the mind. We have
to battle with our very own sources, our own prayers, to
carry conviction and deaden these seductive voices of empty
excitement now so prevalent.

April 24th, 1975
The answer for a life and wrong – i.e. conceited – thinking: I
think the punishment lies in the contraction of the conceit
itself, which forces the soul into a tiny space and makes it
wither. But the final answer we cannot foresee – only I
believe it must be a release, because it will be the truth even if
it hurts, and it will be expanding and joyful in its perfection.

November 3rd, 1975
The negative way is only possible inside the non-
achievement; compromises are forced on us spiritually and at
the same time are denied by us – and this is the source, ever
flowing, of vigorous repentance. It occurred to me that the
hermits went into the desert to save themselves for a *training*
in the Gospel love of non-exclusiveness from the compromises; but always some had to come back to be entangled with
teaching. One could see the Jesus Prayer as that desert retreat,
or the Canons,[1] and when one comes back the teaching is as if
one did not teach, and the defending as non-defending, etc.
But this *double negation* is the innermost core and when the
mind catches up with it then I believe that sense of fear
around the ankles is overcome in its tripping-up power: I
mean a coincidence of the mind and the heart in the search for
Truth; the clear distinction of Reason and reasoning; the true
philosopher against the 'worldly philosopher'. The mind
must be anchored, then one is safe in whatever one does. In a
way, the negative way is the way where the *mind* can in full
vigour participate in work freely within its loved limitations
(because the limitation gives it the freedom of work) and
when one discovers the coincidence with the Gospel, then it
becomes exciting and the Gospel opens wider and wider and

[1] Liturgical poems, comprising nine odes

ever more satisfactory to the mind. Once the consent of the mind[1] is reached, the direction is set and the will flows gladly. All this is my innermost heart.

March 24th, 1976
But what is eliminated is the speculation on things we cannot understand. This gets more and more boring. It is far more interesting to work with the mind inside the field which is given us to work within the imperfect.

June 4th, 1976
I was attracted to Plato, or really just 'coming home', and inside him, the moment Gauss gave me the key in his first lesson. Apart from anything else, I am ever taken in joy by the careful examination of the unreliability of sense perception and its servant rôle to stimulate thinking, but then the soul must retreat upon its watchtower and look up to the ideas. This, of course, set me free to be where I want to be.

August 7th, 1977
Don't worry, it will, in September, be just the right time for you to come. It is, anyway, my own month, a cherished month and there is still a lot of resilience in me when I lie still. The circumference of action is now very narrow but the very heaviness of the past years has lifted and I feel now as if I were walking into or towards a light. There is a little voice telling me all the time that it is all coming to meet me and I begin to look forward to that. I also feel very strongly that everything will be precisely right and according to some precise plan. I also feel the Monastery more solid than in times of darkness, although what now rests on the other two is far too much. But with B. here, we felt how in a moment all could be changed and be full of sunshine. We still laugh and are merry and I would die as lightly and merrily as possible. I so love what Whichcote once said: 'We have only one thing, the consent of our mind; the heart's consent is unshakable when the mind knows why.'[2]

[1] See August 22nd, 1973 (p. 19)
[2] *Disc.* 59; III, 209

III THE ORTHODOX FAITH

Platonic attitude – the Mystery – reality of the
event – repentance – liturgical texts – Old
Testament – tradition – translation

The joy of the Orthodox faith for the thinking mind lies in its
attitude, which is in full harmony with the Platonic attitude of
thought. Platonism, as seen in the Orthodox faith, allows for
lack of fuss in not knowing: we cherish the Mystery. The
attitude is sober, the demand for a life lived in full, and no
ideology: and because the religion *is* a life, we will not lose
the *reality* of our belief, the *reality* of Christ God, the *reality* of
the Gospel in its double movement of here and now, and in
eternity. So, too, as in Plato, there comes in the attitude of
the humility of the hypothesis, the ever beginning again in
the work of repentance, and thus to the work of love inside
the darkness, as seen in the liturgical texts. It is in these texts
that we find the unity of pure thinking and faith. And,
further, this same reality persists into the Old Testament, the
real person of the prophet, and the love of God within his
grieved anger. There is nothing to be afraid of in praying the
Psalms, as in their laments, their cries for vengeance, we
meet our own limitation and, hence, repentance, and the
unfailing trust in the love of God. But what is all this 'bulk'
which we will not discard? We leave nothing behind us, we
alter nothing and all that our Fathers carried we carry as the
greatest treasure. It is the *tradition*, our bulwark against personal fancy, passing enthusiasm, transient fashion. Tradition
is our gossamer web that links each day to heaven. One way
of retaining the tradition in England is to try to ensure that all
our services are available, in careful and precise translation, so
that the continuity of tradition is preserved with the echoes
and cross-references, the repetition of words and phrases,
intercrossed from prayer to prayer, service to service.

24

September 14th, 1945 (G)
Today, writing to Dima,[1] I saw once more how the Russians, with their different constitution from us, make straight for the eternal. The Westerners cannot follow them. I felt that strongly in Dima's letter. They have actually other ways of knowing; they are stronger in their prayer- and heart-knowledge than we are in our head-knowledge. The danger of the purely theological head-knowledge, which easily becomes so hard and untrue, so to speak, the nearer it draws to Truth theoretically, simply does not exist for them. He writes to me that he has no possibility within himself to read the Bible other than praying (as we 'study' it). And yet there is also a danger in this approach; I only sense it, but do not yet see it.

October 8th, 1965
It is a *way*, and a rough one. The faster all the rough things come in, the better. So the more rough waking-up, the better. It is a *work*; to turn it all into joy; first to accept it without fear and then to find the glory in it. Repentance is true only in stillness and peace: – and in joy.

October 16th, 1965 [to Sister Thekla]
I am terribly keen to introduce you into the mysteries of the OT – only then the NT stands out in vigour, beauty, splendour – in its *deepest coincidence* (but not ordinary or on a flat level) with the OT. As to the monastic vocation – it comes out *great* in Jeremiah! – worlds are lying before you to be explored; and it's the plane of my 'competence'.

February 3rd, 1966
The prophets begin pulling. I am hastening towards them. If they switch on their magnetics there are no means of escape. They absolutely hurl me into it – the stormwind of vision.

April 16th, 1968[2]
The Gospel *is present* in all its details; it wants to be lived and relived precisely as if it happened here and now. What a

[1] Father Dimitri
[2] cf. I, May 14th, 1968 (p. 4) and Eastertide 1968 (p. 26)

revelation this was for me when I discovered it! If the shift from 'presence' to 'remembrance' takes place, the devotion and arbitrary choice of feeling are unavoidable.

Eastertide 1968
I had a thought and better put it down! before something else occurs to take it away!! I thought – reading your letter again – that the 'balance and unity' of Cross and Resurrection cannot be found without the 'presence' because the balance is not a psychological condition but a *Person*; therefore inner life and worship are affected if the presence is lost, and by the back door the history part begins to *prevail* in a destructive and far more autonomous way. 'Presence' emphasizes in the reliving of the Passion and all the stages precisely the eternity – and not history – part of the life of Christ. *Because* it has an eternity part it can be *re*lived (though only according to our small measures). And this is so terribly important – the presence of the Cross – not only because Christ raised with the world also his earthly life – *but* because the resurrection can only be lived *on earth inside* the Cross. I say 'inside' and not 'on' because our little passions have their reality only inside Christ's passions.

Resurrection and Cross have both a precise meaning; their unity lies in that this meaning is precisely the same. Thinking through every stage in St John's teaching it is clear: Love is life; Love lived purely, divinely, *on earth had* to be the supreme self-sacrifice, since it had to embrace and not exclude evil as one whole. But Love lived purely *is* Life. And the resurrection is the ultimate irrevocable witness to that.

There was no seed of corruption of which Christ died; he *lived* inside his death. He died a living death. But this does *not* mean any docetism. He died wholly.

And the mystery we shall never fathom. But as far as one can think – even so far it all fits.

Therefore is *the Tomb* so much connected with the monastic life. The unerring, unshakable, holding fast at the living inside the Passion, where it is overcome and the glory – one feels the rising life in trees in February before it shows – is there hidden, but so *truly* as we can on earth see it. Easter we can believe, but the Tomb we can see.

Again it was so overwhelmingly real – and in such unutterable peace that we shall be allowed to die into the peace of *that* Tomb, when we die: and that every partial dying is also into *that* Tomb and therefore holding and bringing new and ever greater revelation of the Life of Christ's death. And it strikes at the life-nerve of men's life – their fear of death – to overcome.

If the grace of our – in a way 'childish' – childlike, sharing in the Passion in Holy Week is taken away, the monastic life somehow, as I see it, loses its centre – its gravitation – its ultimate home; of course it need not, as inwardly anything is possible, but why should a grace of personal presence, or at least the virtuality of it (our making the way ready for it), be thrown away? What to gain? It *is* a childlike sharing, a childlike faith; but if it is, I want to be thus childish.

It is true it should be one *whole* life, but it surpasses the strength of most of us, to live it so explicitly all the year, and the Church Fathers were no fools when they appointed a limited time of forty days and ultimately three days.

I shall never forget the wonder of entering actually into a new life when I discovered that there was a Holy Week to *live*.

And as light broken in a prism, the three days are again brought back in the saints and martyrs, that, in a bearable way Holy Week does stretch over the whole year. It all makes so much sense. The saints as part of the *unity* – in the Person; they are calling, they still witness with their lives that the Mystery goes on, the life-thread is not broken. The *Life* of Christ passes – 'passes over'.

Why – if Christ so wishes – should this Life not converge in a focal point in Holy Week?

December 2nd, 1968
And there is, of course, a great deal of Old Testament work; to dispel *unawares* the God of wrath against the God of love; Law against Gospel, which is nonsense; just by making the texts live and letting the *persons* shine through.

December 11th, 1968
I am certain the 'involvement' in every sense is a lessening, a
barring of the way. The young ones deny the tradition; if it is
given up in order to meet their desires, it will be lost for all
future generations. This is so evident in the Protestant
Churches. Even with the utmost efforts it cannot be
regained. If, on the other hand, we do not answer their
immediate desires and wants, but simply keep true to what
revealed itself as true to us, at least it is there when they want
it. And even in the revolt, they will feel a security if the
balance is held.

May 28th, 1969
The true self-revelation of God is only in the Person of
Christ. His redeeming suffering goes beyond all demands of
merely ethical justice. It is the higher way, which takes the
sting out of innocent suffering. It is ultimate, the ultimately
valid, decisive, divine reality.
    Sola fide. Grace is God coming to meet our feeble human
striving. He perfects in infinite measure what is begun in
finite measure. Is grace thwarted if linked to a human condition? Only if the finite could in any way be set and 'fron-
tiered' against the infinite. And this would be an impious
attempt to limit the divine, make it relative to the creature.

May 25th, 1970
The language [Greek] is ... like a coming home, home
being far, far back in the time of the Apostles, but also home
because now – at the very end – the three mighty streams of
philosophy, OT, and my Orthodox faith – meet.... And in
the back of course is the joy of being able soon to read Plato
again fluently.

July 10th, 1970
Before I went to Archbishop Athenagoras I went again
through the footnotes[1] and had two inspirations:
1) *Faith*: the wholeness of the person because gathered up
into the *causa finalis*.

----

[1] notes on the Cambridge Platonists (unpublished)

Doubt: the divided person. Doubt is never theoretical, always practical. It only torments us when a choice is involved; neurotics unable to act are but an exaggeration of our own divided will.

Now the whole must embrace the parts. Faith must embrace doubt, and train itself in this to get strong, for it is the exercise of directing the parts into the *causa finalis* even before the solution is found theoretically. It is analogous to the mind in the exercise of the first four steps of knowledge.

The gathering up of multiplicity into unity, the unity, yet unseen, for faith as if it were seen.

Faith in a sense is the renunciation of choice.

2) The leading out of faith from mindless coercion (feeling, fear, emotion) *into* the mystery (coercion is the 'myth'), through the critique of reason; of *our* faculties, which will lead to the overcoming of every form of passivity in religion.

By accepting evil as a field of action for faith it is placed into the 'fearful' (for evil) *operation of the end* (how I love St Catherine!), the one thing it wants to avoid.

May 28th, 1971

You see, I believe, what I call Truth is something incredibly different from truth, and probably just as wild. I call truth: the truth that Love (i.e. the divine life, absolute, excluding nothing) can only be lived on earth in the contest of evil; as I describe it in the talk;[1] this is the 'living in eternity', 'living in love' – and the Truth of life is that Love *can* be lived on earth in finite measure; and Christ told us how; he lived it purely; therefore he *is* the Truth – and because Truth is 'Love lived', therefore Truth is a Person. It is *all* back to front. Truth is not an abstract coherence of things, or not only; and therefore you are right, that there is no truth; in that sense. I love John Smith: 'Truth is not a bulky thing, it does not fill many volumes' (not a precise quotation). Things converge into so few words in the end.

January 12th, 1972

... and surrounded by prophets alone in the wild desert of

---

[1] *Eastern Spirituality*, Westminster Cathedral Library

Judah, and the joy – my own innermost joy breaking through again from inside.

The writings might come; as yet I plod my way, as it were, through the backdoor – into the prophet-world.

June 3rd, 1972

I also suddenly thought that there is Tradition backwards: the personal life of the Holy Spirit within the personal life of the Fathers, but equally Tradition forward into the Communion of Saints, again eminently personal. We cannot deny 'Tradition', because we love every motion of the Spirit and every personal expression of our Fathers. Tradition is quite simply a question of love; and our will to abide in time and no-time; freely moving forwards and backwards, no longer so narrowly bound within space and time.

June 4th, 1972

You see 'traditional' teaching for us is a living intercourse with the persons. It is not just doctrine, and it will never go into words. But this means giving away our secrets.

December 2nd, 1972

Yet, we do *not*, and never will, understand our work as 'ecumenical', that is as for the sake of 'making contacts', or of 'explaining Orthodoxy to the West', or, indeed, of any form of vis-à-vis the West, as if the Orthodox faith, which claims each person's life wholly, were 'an interesting piece of information or inspiration to fill up gaps'. We understand our work quite simply as a firm, and not a softly tolerant, witness to the Orthodox understanding of the Gospel, which – as I see it – perhaps alone of all Churches does not see faith as opposed to knowledge, but as opposed to doubt, and, therefore, can courageously face not-knowing in every realm, and can overcome doubt by faith, without disclaiming the right to thinking. It is the unique charisma of the Orthodox of the Together of eternity and history, Mystery and event, which could solve, if at last it were seen, the impasse in the life of faith of many today.

September 18th, 1973

... and have always the long psalm readings in this form, inside the Greek offices, which we also have sometimes in English. But we like the *harmony* of rhythm between the two languages, thus forging a link to the sources, that when the changing to English comes, which is inevitable, it will be, at the core, linked with the Greek in our hearts, and perhaps also as in the 'soil' – as we dig it into an Orthodox soil by praying.... I love best Psalm 80. *Often* I pray the first lines and they hold, what Hooker once said of the prayer of the desert Fathers: in piercing brevity – many pains. And Psalm 44 with the acute sense of martyrdom in it. Psalms 90, 91 and 102. And very much 132, 84, and the pilgrimage psalms 120–134.

October 24th, 1973

Confession is an everlastingly open question. I feel what you are doing to be right. For short periods, I had years ago very frequent confession. I do not really advocate it although I see your point. I think it is just as important and relevant as frequent absolution – to learn the unceasing repentance in the *carrying* of the total inadequacy every minute in front of Christ, very high and very direct, standing there, we in front of him, our Judge. To make the End-point and the abiding in it an *attitude* is the release into a freedom, which we only can have at the end and from the end. Weave the end into the way – that never one is without the other; and at the end hold your breath. This is the task – and the way towards the fulfilment, for in the knowledge of the non-fulfilment we, as it were, make a huge leap into the 'realm' of fulfilment, as unprofitable servants – the cross of Christ our 'boast'; i.e. we abide in the 'foolishness' as far as we are concerned, fools in every respect.

November 21st, 1973

... the unity of doctrine and worship, because we cannot talk *about* Christ, when he is just here, with us in hell. So theology *must* be in the presence of Christ, we do not have the notion of a glorified Christ, as opposed to Christ incar-

nate; nor Christ against God mediating. Christ destroyed sin,
not the punishment of it.

Feast of the Transfiguration, 1974

But meanwhile a prophet book is in the process of being
born. The prophetic attitudes of the Orthodox liturgical
texts. The non-concern for time, the identification on many
levels, the immense emphasis on the Person, each one – and
All. Always Persons. The jealous guarding of the *Event* –
inside and outside time – and much more. Above all the
prophet as the intercessor – not in praying this or that – but
the prophet himself *is* the intercession; as he carries *inside*
himself the people; and intercession means the carrying into
the presence of God explicitly; and so fulfilling partially the
goal of each life.

September 3rd, 1974

One can, of course, not 'take in' and 'take up' nor transfer the
Eastern tradition, as it were, in a gulp. It will be a long
journey of discovery, of patient breathing and living in an
atmosphere, of different 'melody', rhythm, and I would say,
also of a wholly different experience and use of 'time'. Time
and eternity are ever inside each other, and there is not a
thought, which is not 'crossed out', or which does not 'cross
out itself ' in the double movement of progressing time and
standing eternity. So that perhaps the first step into the
Orthodox world is the acknowledgement that in the face of
eternity – in the *personal* standing before the face of Christ,
our God – Judge (always Judge) and Saviour – Christ – God
in his self-limitation, so that we could 'see, hear and touch'
him, and Christ in the unattainable glory – as ONE.

   This is the source of an attitude of faith, *attitude* towards
every event, every thought, specific and often alien, but also
often infinitely longed for, loved and perhaps needed by
western minds and hearts. It is a different experience of reality. Reality is Christ, and Christ alone; and Christ as Person,
as Truth; in direct Presence, to which we are called up to
'attend'; and Christ as the Communion of Saints, wholly one
in heaven, earth and hell, because there is nothing that ever
can be outside of Christ; and on every infinitesimal space of

earth, and of hell, there rises up the Cross of Christ, which links earth and hell to heaven, eternally, inseparably and finally. So I see a forest of crosses – a forest of expectation and glory inside the suffering and torment and contortion of beauty – of love.

September 17th, 1974
Anglicans come to us often grievously distressed at the New Theology forced upon them and what they even believe taken from them. The unrest is great because of the Charismatic Movement (very noisy and autocratic) and the social work taking the place of prayer, a notion I hate. I smell a cheat. But it runs through the Churches, through the RC too. So of course we are very much 'out' of the fashion, but this does not worry us.

November 13th, 1974
There are a few hints which perhaps might be senseful. Russians, especially genuine ones as Lossky and Evdokimov, presuppose a lot of things, of which we with western minds would not so readily think.

For instance, when they assert a truth violently, it is so natural to them to question it at the same moment, that they would not think of mentioning it. If they talk or write, they are on the discursive level, but know in their *heart*, that there is another base and End, in the face of which no answer will hold, and we lie prostrate before the *Person* of Christ, *tall*, and have nothing to say except: Lord, have mercy, the prayer of the End and the prayer towards the End; this longing of infinite love to learn to love. The mind follows love.

So, if you meet an Orthodox, you must always have that in mind. There is no 'yes' without a 'no' on our human plane. I see here the unspeakable 'grace' of our Church; but it needs a lifetime to explore it. It is exciting. What is the most exciting is the adherence to the Gospel as a 'contemporary' *event*, because here time and eternity meet. This is completely simple; no extrasensorial experience. We just know it *is* and love it so. When, in Holy Week, as monastic custom, we read all the Gospels from beginning to end up to St John 12 in the first three days, our 'feet hurt' of the walking, up to Calvary, to heaven and back again to the beginning. In the crowds, understanding nothing, but allowed to *be there*; quietly slipping into his presence *as* present. It is never the question of an eastern and western mind ultimately. The innermost core is simply 'the attention to the presence of Christ'.

November 30th, 1974
Sr Th. is copying out in writing all our basic translations, i.e. of the structure of all the services. We are also starting an index of uniformity of recurring phrases, so that they can more easily be cross-followed; I mean what is in Greek uniformly the same, and should be an indelible part of one's memory. One immense push towards it is this memory-question. After all the work, we still don't know our services by heart; and this is not right.

December 12th, 1974
I have an idea: one could – in the OT prophetic consciousness – see the integration of the middle sphere into the centre very precisely in the oneness of wrath and love. We *are*, in Psalms, and even in the NT, allowed the warmth of complaint, tears, desolation, and exaggerated joy, i.e. the whole orchestra of the middle sphere plays. And to make the Psalms in the Office aseptic is another twentieth-century folly as *hubris*; and then straight into the mourning of God over his own desolation at loveless response; and *his* orchestra of love and threat playing freely. And he lets us see him so. There is underneath all this, an ineffable tender self-effacement of God. It must be warm. He reveals himself deeply attached to his love. Why not we? This is exciting. God was incredibly 'courageous' to let his Church loose with the Psalms; no fear of the middle sphere; but a direct taking it up into his. And Christ made it abundantly clear that he was unafraid.

January 28th, 1975 (G)
But there is no doubt whatever that during a night in hospital I have been able to work out our specific position within the Orthodox situation in England – not belonging to any existing group or to all – *between* Greek and English, but linguistically more and more turned towards English in our transla-

tion, with Greek hymns. In such a way that the Greek language as the precise, unsentimental Christian language of the NT echoes in the translations and the atmosphere. That is important to us. In that way Greek and also English can at all times feel at home, without loss to our integrity and identity – Orthodox in theology, but not bound ethnically and straining beyond all boundaries in *spirit* and prayer. This privilege I shall not allow anyone to take from me – this 'universalization' which grows wider and ever wider. But with all that, as you know, we stand alone, entirely alone, and are now fortunately far enough away to be found only by people who *want* to find us.

February 11th, 1975
I think we are on a sound track, if by the Canons we can show the Orthodox attitude of *mind* and heart. At last we shall be outside of what could be considered idiosyncratic. Yesterday we were at Vespers quite bowlded[1] over by the force of the Resurrection verses in the immediate presence of the *Event*. Mystery and event, and if the limitation of human reasoning is not found present, the room for the Mystery (in the sober sense) will ever remain untransparent. But 'limitation' for me means the humility to work inside the limitation, joyfully in the poor piecework; not to deny the mind – this is really what I want to have lived for – the work of the mind inside its gladly accepted limitation – and with this goes together the understanding of the self-limitation of God. . . . We were also again and again struck by the absence of the 'ransom' theme. Christ: for us, Love as it *can* in its highest fulfilment be lived and realized on earth. And we trot after him, already taken up from eternity into him, trying to do things precisely as he in a tiny measure, not in order to be saved from wrath, but in order to *see* him and to comprehend. There lies the release. And every awareness of sin is but an awareness of not-sin and a greater comprehension of love. Therefore repentance is the dew of the morning.

---

[1] 'bowlded': an emphatic past tense much favoured by Mother Maria

February 14th, 1975
It was strange how, in the experience of the 'mixedness' – the 'goodness', so-called – wholly disappears in importance, and only the sin remains, infused in all and so ugly. And the immediate relief and impact: he carried the sin of the world as one whole. The new theologians are idiots if they deny that. Where else can we stand? It is all so unbelievably lovely. But nothing is so important than to pray for repentance – because it is like dew on the world and the heart.

February 16th, 1975
I hate sense-images for the faith and such a hard faith as ours – let alone ecstatic madness-image for its fundamental dry austerity. So I rather feel lost to reply.

March 2nd, 1975
And, of course, above all I see the *desert* to blossom – the real, cruel desert, not the idyllic desert beauty – and this means that never will I take anything out of the hands of the 'devil'. Even if in his un-person he unpersonally handed it to me, I should refuse and have it from God alone – from him not as punishment, but as infinite tenderness. And so I see the OT wrath, especially in the prophetic consciousness, as inverted love, and both as love alone. This is so exciting, because in the OT it is so humanly laid out, that one can live it directly. It is warm, imperfect, and wholly spontaneous – unconcerned with the imperfection – and an immense space for wildness in image, and the image is always the reality. The prophets stood at the gap – 'at the bank of the River of Jordan', and they stood where the waves of event and of thought were breaking and had to revert 'to begin again'. And they were looking into the Abyss, always – faithfully, without self-pity, and they were the outcasts; and only as outcasts did they work. One catches the distance of the fool in each one: 'Watchman, what of the night?' It is ever the night, unseeing eyes, unhearing ears, and dumb; but this does not prevent the unceasing labour of standing and looking for the light beyond. Isaiah even integrated the not-being-heard into his own vocation to work. Could he have gone further? The non-success as a command out of the mouth of God,

heard in the whirlwind of union with that which was bigger than himself. There was no room for a programme, a fanfare. Let there never be room; for in a moment the flood which will drown all the land in 'Assyria's march' – it will reveal the sheltering wings – 'with us is God', and what could never be included in a programme will be the Truth – present – whose witness is the privilege of the monk.

Or again, the wide and explicit integration of every unfaithfulness in full human image, fully suffered, and fully lifted up into union. How the prophets knew what repentance would mean: 'to cleave close to me, that they might be my people, my glory, my praise and my priceless treasure', and one would see the threat for the denial of God again as a tender taking of the sin of the people upon himself. That which is the prophet's making, the desolation of going away, turns in the prophet's heart into the work of God, and be it total destruction, if it is God who does it, all is safe, and all will ever be safe – his own work, his own life. God carefully guards the destruction in his own hand, because so it turns into life – in the prophet's vision; and then explicit in Christ.

March 11th, 1975
I think one should begin to drop the notion of 'West and East', which is a lie and ever carries the seduction of idealism and escape into another culture. Western mind *is* capable of dialectic, *humble* thinking, and on that alone rests the understanding of Orthodoxy – or rather, I would say, of the Gospel. No straightline thinking will understand either prophets or parables – nor death/life and life/death convergence.

March 30th, 1975
... we are working much at the English Office for ourselves, and we are now going completely, except for singing and Liturgy, into English; with Greek and Slavonic in the background, like the eternity-beat.

April 24th, 1975
What is important is to get – worming oneself through a lifetime – to the understanding of what we mean by repentance; which is a wholly different thing from what it sounds,

and already belongs ultimately half or more to the other side. But that *is* exciting, and with it goes humility of the *mind* and heart together. And the two things are our beatitude on earth, even if we get hold only of the smallest corner.

July 19th, 1975
Another wrote, after my pamphlet,[1] of the immense gulf in the ways of thinking of East and West – he was a Tractarian – it enters nobody's head that the gulf lies between Aristotelians and Platonists, not 'eastern and western minds'. I have a wholly western mind. And they can't get Aristotelian logic out of their religious orbit of action. The ladder, the ladder, continuation from our side without Yes *and* No, without, i.e., without repentance at the heart of all, being the peace in all things and the joy inside the sorrow.

September 29th, 1975
I woke up today with a glorious thought: are we not really the *fundamentally* evangelical Church? If the Canons are, as it were, the *lived* parables, for instance; also in images. If the Canon images unite into one all the prophetic images, both as persons and as visions of OT and NT, how the Gospel can be lived without watering it down – and how it can never be lived on an earthly moral code, but ever lived upon repentance and joy of heaven. Also, *how* little part punishment and condemnation have, except in the self-judgement; and how lightly Eve gets away! poor darling. Everything is image *without* losing the event; and ever earthly values are as existing acknowledged, denied, and positively transcended, the true creativity revealed. One should follow the images – and so, instead of Byzantine Apotheosis, our Church will reveal itself as Galilee, Jerusalem; and the journeys between. And to prove that from within the liturgical texts would be exciting.

October 7th, 1975
... how can I differentiate between Orthodoxy and myself? Is Orthodoxy an ideology? or a static idol? which has no ears to hear, no eyes to see – as truly some nowadays try to turn it

---

[1] *The Realism of the Orthodox Faith*

into – whom I most readily would call Antichrists, who pro-
fess themselves so loudly the opposite and present a Gospel
with no love – a cruel Church, as cruel as the Inquisition – a
fraud, a lie to every past genuine Orthodox country which in
their days was ever warm and open.... We are working
hard at quite different outlooks – translating the Matins
Canons – and seeing how closely they follow the images of
the Gospel, the reversed values, the interknitting of all the
Bible images – the reality seen as *heaven active on earth but*
unseen. Those martyrs did not *see* their glory, yet the Church
dares to see only that, glorified death, where there was but
terror. But what is so unbelievably lovely is precisely the
integration of darkness: 'I' am never the glorious witness, 'I'
am the misguided wretch, the harlot, the thief, the condemned, ever in the dark – loving the far-away light: Shine
upon me; catch me out of the deep of despair; wrap me up in
your love; shelter me from *your* sentence. There is the not-
seeing, where the seeing is strongest – because it precedes
what immensities there are for which we have no eyes to see.
Were it not so, how poor a heaven were that we are going to,
if it were comprehensible to our earthly ears and eyes and
mind. So I feel myself, in an odd way, intensely confirmed
by the very Canons, in the heart of worship, and see where I
could have shown the bridges to my way of thinking, but I
leave that now to the others. The bridges are exciting. And
more exciting still, how – as with me – the devil cuts a poor
figure, has never any power, where the martyrs' 'not-seeing'
reigns, is cut down like a huge corpse, an ugly shadow. So
wherever in Orthodoxy the devil is given a prominent place,
as is now the fashion, the Orthodox betray their own tradition, not knowing what they are actually supposed to pray
daily.

October 15th, 1975
This is the underlying melody; it would be easy to find
bridges – many – to our liturgical texts, and this will come
out in time. I find it ever more important that the Orthodox
attitude of faith could be shown; for in many ways it would be
liberating and joyful, as the presence of heaven here and now,
almost tangible, is a thing so taken for granted.

October 17th, 1975
Working at some liturgical texts (the Matins Canons) I am
struck how differently we consider what faith is. One might
almost say that faith is – in poetry – standing happily among
the saints and angels, and to *sing* – in or out of harmony is
irrelevant, but to sing and not to fuss about it all being
unseen. And not to have faith would then mean to stand
among them – because one can't escape that – and to sulk.
This is very simplified, but it well accords with my third
diagram.[1] In attitude I find very many bridges to my way of
thinking.

February 28th, 1976
There is, to my mind, only *one* 'spirituality' (I begin to hate
that word) and different participations thereof. I hate the idea
of 'Orthodox' or any other Church's spirituality as merely a
'contribution'. This revolts me. It is ever 'a whole' in different form of expression – ever inadequate.

March 4th, 1977
The descent is painful and begins to feel so, although I can
still think; when called up. We got lately very clearly the
main crossroads we found of Orthodox thinking, when we
landed at Filgrave. That is the unity of theology and philosophy in the Orthodox faith. Where I had that unity before on
the Anglican side, that is now quite excitingly clear and
proved from the liturgical texts.

[The following extract is taken from letters written on March
21st and May 3rd, 1977 to Father Ralph, s.s.m., who has
provided 'crib' after 'crib' for us from the Greek into the
English. The Kelham monks became dear friends when they
settled in Willen in 1973 as close neighbours to Filgrave.]

My Pegasus got going, holding on tight to your translation I
dictated, together with the Greek text, straight off – and the
outcome is a Holy Week of a glorious together of you and
me. I just experimented, inspired by your working, how near
one could venture to get the roughness and abruptness of the

[1] ibid.

Greek. I wanted to see if one might catch thereby the rhythm. The connections I altered are merely an Orthodox idiosyncratic thing of the taken-for-granted crossing of eternity in history: the Mystery, without apology to human reasoning, and without explanation or expansion, in order to leave the spirit free for any explanation which can vary. And for this varying there must be left as much spaciousness as possible. I became very conscious that what in western theology are wearied things reasoned down to death are for us still fresh and green and part of the stylization, which the text shares with the ikons and which obviates the dying a dead death. Also, I tried wherever I could to make the spontaneous free retranslation into the Greek or Slavonic easy – to keep the homely feeling and music still singing. I also realized that our theology is poetry – never hard and fast, is pastoral in a 'from-inside way' and not explaining. The actual being there (at the Offices) and singing always wins over the immediate help to understand. . . . How strongly the Holy Spirit comes to meet one as a Person in the texts, and how soberly the apostolic mediation is kept. I like that subjection and at the same time directness; a fine balance kept. The more one discovers of the texts the more convincing they become, and make one glad. . . . After all the discarding of the Gospel myths, it must be like fresh spring water for you to plunge into the simplicity of our texts which is of course far more subtle than their rationalizing and immanent 'experience'. We somehow manage to believe *through* the inadequate expression on to the other side but in total 'indifferent' simplicity, not taking the things of this world as either final or correct nor ever able to express the fullness of the truth which they express, *and*, being inadequate vehicles, conceal. And this form of believing is a more humble form, less fraud because it has infinite consequences into every sphere of life and achievement; leading ultimately to never-ceasing repentance in the knowledge of non-achievement inside the highest worldly achievement, and from there to the more acute longing for more adequate means of seeing and knowing and loving.[1] The *via negativa* is not the antipode of the *via eminen-*

[1] cf. VI, May 15th, 1975 (p. 80)

tiae, but it takes the *via eminentiae* simply for granted as the immediate field of action, it labours and then crosses it out as achievement in the more acutely perceived and more painfully blinding light of the perfect – the unattainable glory for which we daily, many times, pray. But we do pray for it the more ardently, the more we know it as unattainable and in the 'crossing out' lies our nearest approach to that which is real which rules our life, though ever unseen, and which demands from us these famous outrageous hardships. They chisel us mercilessly. The only comfort is that it would anyway have to be done – if not this, then the other side. So better run this side as far as we can. And in that light – the fact never matters – but only the attitude. Neither the fact of failure nor achievement. That is why I love Thomas More so much. He took that to a furthermost limit, playing the fool all the way along, and when total want was in sight – before his imprisonment – he quietly announced how the family were to go begging and be merry, singing at every door a *Salve Regina*. It did not come to it because he was killed. Even martyrdom he endured *and* in the enduring, crossed out.

June 23rd, 1977
You know, I believe, when we die we shall have one surprise after another, seeing that many values are upside down – as the Parables indicate. And that what matters there, we can never quite know yet. Therefore the emphasis in our faith on 'repentance'. I love that so. There are infinite riches to be discovered in our tradition, and we too are doing all we can to make them accessible.

Write whenever you feel like and on whatever prompts you. Perhaps by writing things will clear up for you, and make you see them anew.

July 14th, 1977
Whenever the doubt of predestination comes up, I think, we should stop abruptly and know ourselves trying to peer into mysteries of *God* alone, which are closed to us. We are meant to *believe through* all darkness that God is Love and only Love, and try to live by that faith alone. If we stop asking the wrong or curiosity-question, we shall see how the Gospel

makes sense within our limited scope. Our scope of reason
and will *is* limited and to know that is releasing. I often think
there was an awe in the disciples when they stressed so the
mystery of Judas. They would somehow not wholly lay it to
his charge alone. Further we cannot go. Never, never can
God want to force you into evil. Evil is not on a level with
love, but always a parasite on good; but its origin we know
not, nor its purpose, it is given to us to work at it and trans-
form it into good within our hearts, by taking it as a blessing,
by asking God to let good come of it. As you cannot *know*,
believe and trust. . . . Thinking and thinking purely, without
selfish motives – 'wherever the Logos will guide you' – is a
glorious thing; and there is for the Orthodox a clear distinction between merely human reasoning and *Reason*. The liturgical texts talk of the reasonable thief, the reasonable flock, all
the time. It is a Reasonable Church just because it knows of
the limitation of human reason and love and will, and finds
its glory in repentance, i.e. the knowledge that 'truth is greater than we are' – and that Love and Truth are inseparably
one – of the same substance. Therefore it is a glorious Church
and so deeply satisfying to the mind as well as the heart. This
aspect (with the texts of the Matins Canons) might be a help
for teaching. The balance held in the Canons is admirable.

July 28th, 1977
I often think – in the mill of limited human reasoning which
now claims ascendancy over the Gospel – we shall soon be
reduced to the simple confession: *Christianus sum*. In the distinction of reasoning and Reason the Orthodox Church is the
eminently reasonable Church, and once one discovers that,
nothing can touch one's faith *when it is united in heart and mind*.
We have so many mind-prayers, *logikos* – *noetos* must stand
out, even if for western confusion it is ununderstandable; for
us it is not. We preserve the unity of Love and Truth and hold
to that – 'the reasonable thief'. And this, in every particular,
is our monastery's message which we had to preserve intact.

IV PRAYER AND ANSWER

Work inside the darkness – love and trust

The solution, if there is one, will only come in the context of darkness. There is ever the Mystery of the not-knowing, the suffering and the carrying of the partial, but always within the light of the transcendent. It is not possible to fall out of the love of God, nor out of the company of the saints. Any form of spiritual satisfaction can only be viewed with distrust, and so too any demand for satisfaction. The joy is inherent inside the faith (love) which for only this short passage of life can manifest itself in trust.

———————

[No date] 1952
I never get beyond the prayer: Spend my life if there is anything to it. That 'if' is never with certainty answered and would not be if an angel from heaven would say: 'There is.' It can be answered only by God himself and not before the journey's end. And I would not have it different.

July 1953
Trust is the truest mirror of love. How cheap is a love which falls into doubts at every turn. God is so handicapped when there is no trust. He cannot act. This is the greatest hurt. Passing sins can easily be atoned for, but distrust in a far greater measure closes the door and loses time, which is then *really* lost. The loss of time through sin is often only a seeming loss – but with distrust it is a real loss. There is no prayer so true and so dear to God as: 'I believe absolutely everything you are going to do.' Perhaps the only way we can give each

other chances for heaven is to go on trusting others in spite of their deceiving us as often as they like.

July 1954
We cannot waste any time for 'not-suffering'. Too much depends on our suffering whatever we can; the kind of suffering is irrelevant – that is the economy of God and beyond our choice.

[No date] 1956
With every prayer God puts us at a higher window, to look out over the whole world with a wider view and an expanded heart.

[No date] 1959
The Jesus Prayer works so gently from inside. I mean, what is the end of the prayer, but a *constant* look towards heaven. And the more we weave prayer into daily life and every action, the more will it be a transforming power of love. Fighting for your rights will never do. After all, it is an untrue thing, we *have* no rights – as Christians; and life becomes interesting and exciting only from that time when we have found out *this*: that we *can* die. An inward death, day after day, and over and over again, is a form of life, which we *can* live; and to discover this is a thousand times more of worth than any amount of earthly happiness and comfortable well-being.

July 1961
The total peace of a total acceptance of suffering *is* joy and beatitude.

When a thing is accepted, it is redeemed.

August 1965
Since we do not know the final cause, we have no means of an answer in the final sense. I see the answer in a practical way: to unite ourselves inwardly to the transfiguring light – a faith which is almost vision, when glory comes into sight, *malgré tout*.

October 7th, 1965
You see, going slowly and sleepily is in fact racing full speed; because the less one does, the shorter and straighter the road. Sleeping means short cuts and giving God a free hand instead of constantly bothering him with our short-sighted question-ings. 'Thinking' is something quite different, i.e. awareness to the presence of the *mind* of God.

October 11th, 1965
It seems to me – after what Christ has told us – that we *should* ask things in prayer, when we are in need, simply, directly – and selfishly.

October 12th, 1965
It seems to me that we *should* pray directly, simply and hum-bly bringing our need and perplexity always before God who told us to do so even 'impertinently'. 'What will God do if the unjust judge could not resist?' It is necessary to learn 'selfishness' in order to learn to know God deeply, inti-mately.

February 6th, 1966
I always pray over beyond my utter despair of physical inadequacy to how I wished I could pray. . . . What will it be, one day to arrive and to find oneself in an adequate world – unhampered by creaking nerve-ends.

October 1st, 1967
When he[1] listened he was very still, and at one point he even asked questions – about doubt being the passage that must be endured if the solution is to come 'heavenly'; no decisions, but waiting; no plans, but waiting and suffering the agony of blindness and not-seeing, not resigned, but in the alert expec-tation of the heavenly solution and way. And how every *human* decision led to new partial decision, had to be kept up by more and more decision; every act of impatience kept up by more blind impatience. This he eagerly took in.

---

[1] a young Orthodox Frenchman who later became a monk

October 1967 [to a woman who asked for guidance on prayer]
If you go to sleep with the Jesus Prayer, I think it is an
excellent way of going to sleep, and one day you will find
yourself waking up with it as well, and that is still better. I
never found anything near hypnosis, etc; it is a call, a breath
of joy or thanksgiving for the Presence, a simple and short
acknowledgement that in prayer the presence that matters is
not us but God, that we have of ourselves terribly little to say
which makes sense. Praying the Holy Name, we pray the
whole Gospel, we place ourselves in it and live it, more and
more until it becomes our very own life, our home and our
true end wherein death turns into life. . . . Prayer is a labori-
ous, often a lost and dark and a hidden road which we see
backwards better than forwards. This sense of blindness, of
not knowing – 'Is one praying or not?' – this torment of not
knowing what prayer is, is meant to be, it is all part of the
life, the puzzling, crucified life of prayer. There are no high
roads, and any 'divine office', any set-out prayers, are merely
an acknowledgement of this – a loving and humble taking of
our low little place in the vast choirs through all the ages of
Christians who wanted to pray and lived in the hope that
God would make prayer of words uttered often in darkness
and into darkness. This *life*, this persistent enduring of the
senselessness of our words, matters. . . . I often think of St
Thérèse of Lisieux, how great she was when she said that we
could only have such a short time when we can show God
our blind trust as a proof of our true love. Soon we shall die
and *see*, and never again not-see; and seeing, it will be easy to
love. But in not-seeing, in not knowing what prayer is, there
lies the supreme joy of love, the unique grace of our earthly
existence. . . . We are not at home, we are on the way. We
are not in the day, but in the night; the day is coming, but not
in this life. We live our life inside the solution, and yet we do
not have it because it is too great; we could not grasp it. True
prayer is what the angels and saints do in heaven, we are too
small for it, our minds do not stretch far enough, our hearts
are not wide enough. *But*, in suffering the lack, we come
nearest. We have it not, but we humbly and very slowly
grow towards it. One day we shall be able to pray, pray
without ceasing. One day we shall pray and never again cease

to pray; and then we shall know, *not* before.

Don't worry about heresies, pride, and all those silly things, just *go* and live and *be*. It is enough for God to know; we never do, nor are we meant to.

April 18th, 1968

I wonder if faith *inside* continued doubt, and the *bare* enduring of doubt *is* not faith in its most tender and true humility; the inseparable mixture of suffering and joy, which is the only way to live glory on earth.

August 7th, 1971

I thought yesterday, that my way of 'ruling' is to 'carry' the conflicts; not to force solutions.

August 16th, 1973

Oh yes, I often think, what bliss life would be if one only *knew* what is wanted, but as for me, the waiting and waiting for 'seeing' the next practical step, has grown into pretty large proportions; but the very strange thing is that together with the peaceful agony of waiting, there also goes a sense of having treasures of comfort, gradually growing unawares; because the waiting is so strongly towards a solution, so that it invisibly is already here inside the waiting, making the darkness light from inside.

[No date] 1974

Your letter has deeply moved me, and quite spontaneously I wished Father Sofrony's advice could be followed, simply, quietly, to rest in prayer and solely to attend, deep-inwardly, unrelenting and unceasing, to the *presence* of *your Lord* and *Master*, that is the immediate presence which ever holds and guards you, minute by minute, in ineffable love. And this attention would be a witness of peace.

But I do not know you, nor what lies behind or may lie before you, so what can I do but express my deepest sympathy and assure you of our continued prayer for yourself and your family.

June 28th, 1974
Never worry if you can't pray; it means nothing.

July 2nd, 1974
We have all waited, perhaps past endurance. But things always happen like that. And then suddenly the way is free and the spirit and the whole being rejoices.

September 3rd, 1974
Any other questions, of a spiritual rather than factual manner, which you may have, I will gladly try to answer – or rather 'not-answer'. I *do* believe in questions, but I do *not* believe in slick readymade answers. It is a journey, the soul must go it step by step. And Christ leads the soul. But the questions might be directed into forward-going questions.

November 13th, 1974
I am, at this moment, almost free except for journeys to Leeds Hospital for two days. Cancer of the spine, which hit me two months ago. But that makes no difficulty, if you wished to see us; except that, in the constant inner 'presence of death', answers fly far, far away.

November 30th, 1974
One could really equate 'loving properly' with 'suffering well' – so the course is lucid and logical. Only I complain a terrific amount.

December 12th, 1974
The heaviest part for me is ever, and in every smallest detail, the struggle for clarity. If heaven is to 'see', what this will mean! This trudging on from darkness to darkness, never seeing where one is going, and always help just *past* the mark of endurance! But, at least, in this way one need not reverse and lose time, if one waits long enough.

December 19th, 1974
You know how I can be thrust off my own innermost concentration, and often long years seemed wholly wasted – ever

away from explicit prayer. But the not-fighting, perhaps, has
turned it into a work. Most of all the suffering of not being
able to pray is prayer, if the longing is there. So *I* live, and I
simply believe it in darkness. It is far more important to
endure darkness than enjoy light. It makes one grow and
overcome fear and this may be our – the monks' – most
important work.... I can never pray properly except in a
calling for help day and night for us all, but very much a
baby-calling.... I believe praying is still a form of fighting
on a worldly level – from us to God – then there comes a
time, whenever that is taken from us – perhaps we then cry
for help from inside God – if we could see. But the not-seeing
belongs to it. If we saw, we should only make still sillier
muddles. If we could see! Just think *what* we should see. We
should not know ourselves for joy and also perhaps for laugh-
ing at our own anguishes. Once, in the Abbey, I felt the
saints thinking, We should get them through, if only they
were not sad so easily; but then, what does 'so easily' mean in
their standards! They have more fun than compassion, I sus-
pect!

December 23rd, 1974
I wondered, the other day, whether there comes a state when
the cry for help for us all – day and night, which is my way of
praying – is one day a cry from *within* God – more explicitly
so, and then we feel even less that it is so, and more and more
severed, but inadequate to spiritual 'seeing' – the darkness is
perhaps already the too bright light – and if we were to see
more, we should only make a worse mess of it – and so our
eyes are closed and we endure the aridness of a way wholly
different in essence from past experience and joy of spiritual
discovery. So much seems irrevocably past and the future a
firmly, tenderly, deliberately closed door – for our protection
against ourselves.

January 10th, 1975
Why are you thinking you should see always? For so short a
time we are able to *prove* our love by living and believing in
love, inside darkness and ever not seeing. Soon we shall see,
and never not-see again. We shall be visibly embraced by

love and learn to work accordingly. And life on earth will then look very different. Of course, I want to wrap you up like a babe. But as I cannot – you just must be brave. I am not frightened for you. Nothing can harm you. But, I know, you could turn to joy; turn sorrow to joy inside you and find glory. It does cost one's life, but that means nothing. That is what is our duty and calling. And still we are unprofitable servants. So, be unprofitable, inside your desolate work, as it must seem to you. An hour of solution will surely come, and 'come speedily' in heavenly timing.

February 26th, 1975
You know, I think all the fuss made of human suffering is again a confusion of the *causa finalis* with the *causa efficiens*. Suffering is just simply our work on earth – and however we creep through it, we are unprofitable servants, and there is no solemnity about it; no reward waiting. The work itself is the reward.

March 11th, 1975
It is a strange thought that Christ did not teach his disciples to pray. St John did. In exasperation and perhaps impatiently they had to drag it out of him, and whatever the 'Our Father' is – compared with the desert nights when 'he drew apart' – they got a formal answer.

April 8th, 1975
... only get the access inside yourself free. Then your work and daily life could freely *live*; and I know you can do it. I was, at the most decisive time, terribly worried that a jump might not be, and never be, the solution; and only defer it further. There is no such thing as 'a solution' on earth without, or rather, outside the acceptance of, the most bitter suffering *as* a solution. This would be such a redeeming, such an opening and budding forth of heaven.

June 10th, 1975
I often wonder what the saintly serenity of 'leaving all to God' really means, and what it never means. Achieving it wholly on the level of love, I never get there in material

decisions, which ever and ever drive me through a mill of
doubt, of what is the solution.

September 8th, 1975
There are grand fighters who *can* pray, and get everything
they pray for. They do not doubt. I also do not doubt, but I
would ever and ever subject to doubt any petition of mine.
And apart from just loving, I believe I have only one prayer,
'Make it come right' and 'right' means true *sub specie aeternitatis*. I just never achieve taking any of my life seriously in
that ultimate sense.

October 1st, 1975
Solutions cannot be pulled down from heaven; I wish I could
see – but that would be no good, because it must grow from
inside. . . . Follow the road gladly. It hurts a lot, and matters
nothing, the hurt. But turn away from this fascination of
evil. It is in your way, more than any other thing. It keeps
you captive as if it were a reality, it feeds your senses nega-
tively with sense of damnation; the Deceiver. Look away.
Long you have been found. You are loved, you are spoiled,
seen from heaven. And then you lament. So go on lament-
ing, but I never stop telling you that one day you will laugh
at yourself. Laugh now! There *is no* such thing as an
Orthodox-mediated Christ. This is false teaching. Christ is
sovereign, he needs no such mediation. You limit him, your
inner sense-perception likes it better so, understandably, but
this is not all.

October 23rd, 1975
Turn the whole story round. Look, it seems that for this
while it is your task to endure what you feel as exile and
desolate deprivation. But what do you know about heavenly
measures, where it may very well turn out – all this spiritual
trial – as the superabounding grace of your life, if you only
would take it as a blessing, as immense love, as love with no
hedges, no limits, no bounds – as love from your own Lord
who guides you lovingly by the hand through desert land, to
a destination you can now not see, but out of which you can
never fall. You are attached to it by unbreakable eternal cords

of love. But from you it is demanded, to believe that it is love, and never, never take a crumb out of the hands of the devil. No, not a dram of fear. He must find nothing in you. Turn away, *be* frightened, but never look at the fiend. You are defeated if you do – and winning if you see only Christ. But if, with the best will, you will not find that trick, then you still are safe. Because all that gorgeously arrayed evil is but like a silly smoke before your eyes – and can do nothing. It may look like destruction, it is not.

Why can you not take your famine as being fed? It means so clearly that your love lives, that it has but to wait. The famine *is* love *and* being loved. Rejoice over it. And don't flop like that after every joy, home and blessing you receive seeingly. There are immensities you do not see. Open your eyes, they are all around you.... I just *can* not share the prayer enthusiasm; prayer is ever a failure, but an ever-worked and worked-at failure. The Spirit will be *suffered* through and through – turned into glory, but the way goes through the Passion on earth, because there is no other creative way of following Christ. A gigantic cross planted in the innermost being, where it hurts most and the definite call to 'grow up'. Up to what?

December 11th, 1975
As to the Jesus Prayer, the chief concern for me has ever been the *personal*, intimately personal connection with Christ's *presence* – not 'in the heart' so much as facing me; a *full* presence. And to the *attention*, awareness, love, of that presence which, with or without my attention, is there, immediately close, to that, for which inattention is a gross discourtesy, but ever forgiven discourtesy. I trained myself by the Jesus Prayer, which then more and more let every earthly reality be taken over *personally*, be absorbed into that which is ever outside my own grasp, or will or power. This is the cure for desolate loneliness, but it needs a steady, *simple* awareness. Nothing elaborate, only an ever-repeated glance of love, of wanting to love, wanting to pray. And this presence outside then becomes one with the wide, wide land within, which I call the centre and described most intimately in *Sceptrum Regale*. So outside and inside transcendence become one and the

mature person can emerge, deeply and securely rooted in the
transcendent wide distances towards which we are fast moving.

After Easter, 1976
... all this controversy, this way and that, so empty and
emptying. *Live* Love, wherever, however you can and the
Spirit will be there abundantly, but it will *not* release you
from suffering. That is part of our work on earth. Can you
not connect, intimately, your inner mourning with the Passion of Christ? – and just carry it – as you do, without ever
hoping for release; then one day the very carrying may turn
into fulfilment and joy. The joy is waiting inside the suffering.... Can you not *rest* in Christ, rest in love in his Passion?
This Holy Week, the Passion was so much home, so much
our own, so much my and our life – but the Resurrection was
the *work*[1] – a work right outside our own, and the passing
through so outside our capacity and yet so immediately upon
us; where life and death are so near, so immediately there,
and *all* depending on Christ alone, trampling death down by
death.... I had, in my youth, so much of prayer *groups*, that
it is just not my way – and has no attraction to me, except
inside the Offices, so rich in heaven; and oneness with it; and
as yourself, I would never, never sever the Holy Spirit from
the incarnation in the widest sense and from my Lord and my
God. Otherwise I would see the danger of an ever-emptying
syncretism with the eastern religions, whom in themselves I
approach with an open mind, but not as mine.

July 14th, 1977
I just got an extract of Dr Moodie's book *Life after Death*,
where he concludes that we could cope better with life if we
knew more of that. But it would be a lot more sense to trust
into the dark, and inside the dark, that God *is* Love, and then,
when the time comes, have the gentle welcome and 'Life seen
inside the Truth', i.e. inside Love infinite – than demand
proofs of it now where we have a unique chance of proving
our love for God inside the doubt and uncertainty.

[1] cf. Introduction, May 16th, 1976 (p. xlii)

November 9th, 1977

The other thing is that because of 'suffering-praise' there is no way of taking each other's suffering away, because it would mean taking the true work, the true love, away. And this is the harder part of the story and the more arduous part and so contrary to 'social Christianity' which seems to me the furthest departure, if the weight is put on it as central. Never can one put the true Gospel standards upon a group – as one can upon oneself – and the group to take the lead will deprive us of that demand which gives us the strength and the joy. But the second would flow easily from the first and back again to the second.

V MONASTICISM

Monasticism may only be lived purely on the philosophical/religious acknowledgement of its limitation. It should be recognized as the piecemeal, partial work, with no justification other than that of the compromise, within the consent of the mind, to work in repentance on a tiny patch of ground. The monk must ever begin again and again, and whatever he does, he remains the unprofitable servant.

Yet, within the minute-to-minute acknowledgement of its own limitation, monasticism has something to offer of its own peculiar flavour: a monk has no family, no social commitment, and, therefore, as long as he is prepared to remain a-social, without claim or obligation for himself or his brothers as another or better 'family', as long as he does not meddle in outside affairs, he may become a home for all. The monk may freely learn to die to his middle sphere, and, with no need for self-defence, take up the work of love. And, only in this dying, the *Staretz* may take his place.

[No date] 1952
One must never forget that on the human side a monastic life is the desert; on the spiritual side, the Communion of the Saints in heaven.... If the desert character of the monastic way is forsaken, then falls the highest chance of silence within community, and for God to speak; although, of course, for those who merely suffer under it, God can speak in the wildest noise, and one need not fear for that. He can at any time let a veil fall all round so that the soul is in the desert and before God alone.... Now I need silence and not communication with others, that I am effaced for all the others; in case

56

I should ever have to help others. I know, at least, to take just the opposite line in monastic teaching – the *inner* silence, which sets in heaven *the* great treasure, waited and longed for, and here the *longing*, for *that*, and perhaps not much more except love in faith, and the joy of proving it by that 'only faith'. . . . I often wonder why religious seem to need always those high-pitched assertions about their own vocation and life; as if they lived the heavenly life explicitly already and as if every small victory were or should be in the eyes of God of a value of a different order than the battles fought outside. I say NO, a thousand times. . . . We never know *before* we get the final answer whether there is anything to it or not. It is all in faith, and where faith tears its bounds itself and calls itself heaven, there it loses all. The uncertitude is over the whole realm of religious life, over everything. There is no sacrifice, or any act of love, of which we *know* otherwise than by faith, that God can accept it. And within this realm of expectancy of the last day there widens for us a paradise, a *safe* and appropriate paradise of love, and I suddenly realize it is this which the Fathers call fear of God, and that we are 'worms', and *how* they emphasized it, and there is a great and glorious *Jubilate* in my heart that they did; and that this fear is not over-reached by love, but it makes love safe and gives it all chances. Because in that expectancy we can say: whatever thy answer will be, we still love every word of it, even were it a full rejection, this would not take away our love; there all is safe, because all joy is God himself, all glory he himself and nothing for our successes: 'The sanctity is God.' We gain more if we take the pitch low and take it always as a grace, a very rare advantage, the religious life, and that we are *always* in debt towards those outside. . . . It is always strange that there seems to be an importance in that *bare* bearing of the incertitude; and that in solitary life this is a thousand times increased, where any act of charity or any success is renounced and nothing remains except to bear one's own empty hands, empty, empty even of the smallest act of 'love seen'. I often pray: there is nothing to my life, but neither is there any other possible life, and I am glad there is nothing, because I could not bear the thought of ever thinking it of high value . . . not to put any emphasis on the simple obedi-

ence which is only an *instrument*, and *so* to overcome self –
unawares, otherwise, whenever there is an effort of perfection, self comes in the other way round. There is no ascend-
ing except by *de*scending; choosing simplicity and *forgetting*
all ends, even that of self-perfection; forsaking even the end
of the beatitude of contemplation on *earth*. We have heaven
before us and eternity, we can sacrifice everything, even
explicit prayer – we *can* let go everything, God keeps it safe,
what we long for as if it were.... True stability on earth is
the humble acceptance of having no end of our own and of
having not even to *see* where we go, it is really the *repose* in
the will of God; and the trust that he makes us see it; and
where we see it not, God turns our mistakes into his own
will, and therefore we never fall out of God. The wedding-
garment of the poor is something tried on every day and
ready in heaven; and it is the heart expanding into the joy of
God; which is the positive expanding into God and overcoming of self.

April 3rd, 1955
One unmistakably sails down into lower waters if one de-
prives the mind of solitude.

September 15th, 1965
In two words you gathered up my whole life: pain and joy.
And this is the mystery of my monastic austerity: to endure
to live love in heavenly measures while still on earth, without
compromise, without fear; to endure the sharpest pain and
feel and behold the unspeakable joy and glory all in one, as
inseparably one. And this forms us and shapes us like a
refiner's fire far more austere than any obedience and more
effectively and more truly. It moulds the heart, without our
knowing how, to fit the love which they live in heaven. Here
I see our preparation for death: to learn to love like that.

October 8th, 1965 [to Sister Thekla, for the monastic foundation in Filgrave]
As long as it is a *skete*,[1] we shall work with all our might,

---

[1] two or three monks gathered round a *Staretz* (or Elder), living a life of
desert seclusion

because this will be a time of grace, when we are spared of people. There will certainly come a time, when people will come streaming in, and then we must be very brave and deeply rooted in prayer and inner silence. It is so strange how strictly on the Orthodox monastic pattern our way now goes on; I think of all the Fathers, who withdrew into the *skete*, and their community lost them and mourned, but the blessing was always greater in the end than if they had stayed. . . .

I feel exactly the same about family worship. The Church is the place where these bonds are in a sense suspended: a release, and each one a whole personality by itself. I would therefore never call a community 'family' – it is a sharing in the Communion of Saints – *and* at the same time the loneliness of the desert. The desert must be present. I felt that through all my monastic life very strongly. . . .

To see the world, while yet inside it, with monastic eyes, is a very revealing experience. I had to wait in this condition over one year and also found it grim; but I would not miss the time; it was a time of extraordinary inner alertness, as for you now; of excessive longing and insights. They are precious. . . . Please, I beg you, do sleep and eat as much as possible. I am *certain* about it. . . . It is a form of humility to accept this. Our human frame is frail; and it is humiliating how little Spirit it is able to endure; but sheer vanity not to accept this.

October 12th, 1965 [ibid.]

. . . this beginning, when the foundations of *our* form of monastic life must first be found and laid and consolidated, before anyone from outside can possibly intrude. *Then* we can open ourselves wide to any demands, but *not* in the beginning. . . . It will be a *skete* and not a monastery at the beginning; and it should be small; not big – not suggesting that we are expecting people. We are the foundation stones and we must allow God to put us into that place which he chooses, and how he chooses, before there can even be a thought of building and expanding. It will be a way very much contrary to public 'opinion' on *all* sides, but a witness to Orthodox unwillingness to compromise, to Orthodox monastic tradition of 'retreat' and working 'from inside': to

Orthodox reliance and faith in the power of the Spirit, which
we need not help on with our human, plausible means.... I
feel in a direct and vigorous guidance and follow it with a
heart full and full of joy and inner freedom.

October 16th, 1965 [ibid.]
About homelessness – I am not a 'tramp-nature' outwardly,
who walks off one day. It is the inner condition which is *in*
you as well, and therefore gives me the inner freedom I need.
We are *one* homelessness together, and therefore also home
for each other; but not pretence that earth could ever be
'home' or more than a *pre*-existence to heaven.... [1] We now
go ahead with courage and deep inner conviction; and above
all 'alertness'; totally *disponible* to whatever God wants us to
do.

February 6th, 1966 [ibid.]
Perhaps we shall find a very silent rhythm – it must be silent –
almost breathlessly silent – we have a certain time and must
use it to the full – use every minute of it – in an 'erect silence'
– a fierce attention – like a watchtower. (Plato called the
philosophers the watchdogs of the gods.)

March 8th, 1966 [ibid.]
We want to go by the desert Fathers – and just listen most. Be
very still and make it a work to listen.... The life must
grow from *inside*, and we shall have a privilege which few
monks have had that we may let it grow freely and with no
fear lurking anywhere – heaven all around, and the assent to
suffering total. It is so strange when heaven becomes so
active – so explicit – that one can hold it in one's hands, as it
were – and need only follow.

[No date] *1966*
The Abbey has given me a little Hermitage in North Bucks,
when my first disciple fell from heaven – after three months
she was already clothed by the Bishop as my novice in the
desert tradition. The Abbey gave us *all* we needed. We built

---

[1] cf. VII, January 4th, 1975 (p. 92)

our 'cave' in the wilds of N. Bucks, surrounded by fields and cows; and have a lovely little chapel, and on the top floor we built our retreat – where we write, pray and write – *semper scripsit, semper oravit*.... We have a little wood (two acres) and pheasant in it, and many squirrels ... with a huge Russian wooden cross, which dominates all; and is directed towards the chapel corner. The place seems full of saints and stillness and peace.

[No date] 1966 (G)
The house gets more and more like a monastery in arrangement. We first thought to adapt it to the guests; then came an old nun and we changed the guest rooms into cells, so that they are much more beautiful. The two big carpets which we bought with the house and which never ceased to smell of cats now lie rolled together and covered in the refectory, and look like a giant grave of a forgotten crusader.... In the pressures (from 'outside') and the material questions and anxieties, it is good to get old and to watch out for the end. One does simply not allow oneself, as an old nun, to be disturbed by sorrows or influenced by ideas of bishops, and oppressed.

November 17th, 1967
And only in their death are the monks the challenge to the world, not in their life; in their willed death-life which no man can touch, because beyond death opposition has no meaning, it reverts into itself and collapses.

December 10th, 1967
So often in the monastic life time goes and goes for what it has no right to go, theologically. And it is hardly satisfactory to say that it is meant so, or the austerity. It is *not* the answer, though I know no better one myself.

February 7th, 1968 [to Father Barnabas, who celebrated the Divine Liturgy for us in the early days of Filgrave]
We develop steadily and clearly towards the initial and founding vision of being *desert* mothers; the pattern becomes clearer and clearer; we therefore integrate the scarcity of sacraments

into this our monastic life very directly, so that we do not feel
neglected. But it was a *lovely* thing to get such a loving and
ready answer to come when we need it, though it is such a
long journey, and we thank you from all our heart.

April 3rd, 1968
Homelessness, and no rest, *is* the meant condition of Man,
stripped of the comforting fringes of the senses (as in *Sceptrum Regale*). The Truth of Man is from one solution to
another and none ever final because he is in the 'becoming',
i.e. in the imperfect. Rest is perfection, and only as we participate in the perfect have we rest, and the works *follow*. I
believe this is in a strange way the monastic idea, that works
follow if the rest is growing.[1]

April 10th, 1968
You need never have *any* fears about gossip or offence where
we are concerned.
1) We are happy enough that gossip never, never even
reaches us. I despise it to such an extent that – if it did – I
should not hear, let alone believe it.
2) It is wholly impossible to *offend* me. The word does not
exist in my vocabulary in any language – as little as does
'disappointment'.
3) You can trust me and us implicitly and absolutely without
any insecurities; or fears.

April 11th, 1968
It is really a liberating theme; 'rest' as work, and the foundation (so solid) of the contemplative life; in the Benedictine
form it is in the Rule as second nature, joining up even with
Adam, the turning-back of the turmoil of effort into rest, the
living of heaven on earth; the drawing out of the line of joy in
suffering, or suffering as joy, labour as rest, as the highest
form of creativity. On yet another level, the messianic age as
the ultimate Sabbath, where rest does not follow work, but
works spring and grow from rest, as light radiates, effort-
lessly.[2]

[1] cf. IX, May 1st, 1967 (p. 119)
[2] ibid. Cf. VI, [no date] 1952 (p. 73)

July 31st, 1968

I said there was no justification for it, and that the monastic life was the uttermost limit of that situation, which could not be justified in any earthly or even earthly-spiritual terms. That it was the testifying that it is possible to *live* inside the doubt, doubt of the very essence of our work and being, and doubt of which the solution is *voluntarily* renounced and thrown into the hands of God, and not peered into curiously every other minute . . . she felt a freedom which she loved. It is, perhaps, the freedom which comes from the acceptance and total integration of doubt into the life which gives to them a space of protection against, or rather, within, their own less explicit doubts.

October 22nd, 1968

. . . and I am always so filled with gratitude for the *security* I then experienced, surrounding me on all sides;[1] and only in that security could I now enclose 'securely' and safely the utter non-security of the monastery life. It is as if all the strength had mounted up into food for the forty days' journey. But I also see what force such security is and how needed for beginners, not because they are weak, but because they must grow and want to grow. . . . Here I am living in a sort of ship which skirts the frontiers of the world. But the ship, of course, is not me, I could never steer such a course, and never do I know what command will come from the captain. I never lived so much in a journey as I do here, and never was there so much the sense of non-possession.

December 11th, 1968

It makes me happy that you so thoroughly see the way of the thesis; it is like the integration of the philosophy explicitly; and of the way to the monastic life which lay through the thesis. . . .

St Basil is fierce about it. Access must be of the hardest. If they are welcomed and wanted, this is not a release for them, but a constriction, because they never then have the certainty that they wanted it, and when later difficulties arise, this

---

[1] the Abbey years

initial mixture of the two desires (of being wanted and wanting) can then very easily topple over into a feeling of having
been forced – though not rightly. But for the beginning it is
necessary, too, not to be desired, because it mars the direct
confrontation with God, which, I think, is a necessary thing
which should be at the foundation. It goes wholly against any
natural family bonds, where the being wanted gives life to
the child. The not-being 'wanted' (though of course loved)
somehow gives the challenge of a free decision at every future
step, and the joy of choosing.

January 15th, 1969
I had a strange thought about the failure of Orthodox foundations in the West: because there was no Orthodox ground to
build on. I had an idea that what we are doing is to be, in a
kind of way, *ground*; make ground, a wholly Orthodox piece
of land, and much later something might grow, like a preparing of the field, analogous to the 'tradition' on a different
level.

February 25th, 1969
The same with the contemplative life, which is in itself nearest in essence to a philosopher's life, because it is objective
and carried in the will of self-transcendence. I find no pros-
pect in trying to fight Bultmann, etc. – the only strong bulwark is the contemplative life.

April 2nd, 1970
I feel so strongly that the *land* must be prepared for a monastery; it always was so. The tradition must quietly sink into
the *earth* and also the surroundings. The monastery is for the
people immediately surrounding it. It must belong to *them*, as
a signpost and comfort for them. One cannot go into a country house and be a monastery. It must begin right at the
beginning, a transfiguration in the expectation of heaven of
every tree and every animal and *this*, I feel, is happening.

[No date] 1972
I had always thought the opening up would be when I am
dead – and that I should be spared this terror – but the Spirit is

an unsparing Shepherd. But would we want it easier? I always liked rough paths.

December 2nd, 1972
This morning I woke up with a strong sense of renewed clarity of our work and of the Monastery's meaning. It lies in that ultimate witness to the Gospel, in which our Orthodox faith offers its unique strength and consolation to the world. I see the Monastery's specific work as a witness, stripped of the ethnical warmth and the dear, precious ethnical life. There we have nothing to offer. We have, all three, left our home and are only pilgrims. But this does *not* imply the denial, or even the slightest deprecation, of the Orthodox inheritance which so tenderly integrates the whole width and depth of each people's life and history. It only means that we are 'desert mothers', and, as such, called to meet the world at the 'point without latitude', where the world lies in agony of doubt, despair and panic of fear.

March 15th, 1974
What a strange thing life is. I go quietly, hiddenly, unknown except of two or three all through life, and at 60 this explosion into the USA, Canada, New Zealand, Australia, South Africa – and across all the bounds of the Churches. And inwardly, day by day more, I detach myself from all, on to that one point, where Christ alone is – and alone is reality.

[No date] 1974 [convalescing in Sussex]
This beautiful country makes me feel as if it could never spark off our Monastery – it is too polite.

December 6th, 1974
You once asked me what a *Staretz* is. I see him at the End-point, with a heart warm and tender and vulnerable, ready every moment to be hurt, and yet never stopping at the hurt (except for a groan!), and so ever *young* to love more and more. No rules of perfection except the desire to love and the readiness to die for it and be slandered; and eternally misunderstood. It is the fool – the wisest of men, who will not accept the human values as final, perhaps necessary, but never ultimately decisive.

December 12th, 1974
I was very shaken at Fr B.'s manifesto. I could not believe
that he could be so starved in his own mind, as – as a monk –
to claim warmth and fulfilment. It makes me wonder –
where lies the error in the monastic concept? It can only be in
the idealism of detachment. But where the solution lies for
communities, and more than just persons, and each one
alone, this I shall never know. I don't think the Orthodox
ever did know. They did hold on to the way of the person –
the monk – the disciple; and carried the innumerable muddles
resulting. But Christ himself had his own, and they quarrel-
led enough; and he let them. Detachment can only be the
attention to the transcendence, which immediately carries the
world (according to our measures) in the heart.

[No date] 1975
We must be storehouses of comfort, wholly unreasonable in
earthly terms. I want to comfort completely outside human
judgement – indiscriminately. This is the privilege of the
monk. Let the wise of this world discriminate as to who is to
be comforted and who is not. I refuse.[1]

January 20th, 1975
There is this immovable centre. This is *not* the personal aim
or achievement of the monk, nor any objective aim, but a
person, who has passed through a death to any worldly concerns, good or bad. *But* again this is a stringently dialectical
way. To have died here means to exert every pain of working
well in this very 'died-to' field; working with all humility and
effort. And this twofold movement, of living towards
beyond and yet from beyond, gaining the impetus of zealous
and *loving* carefulness in the smallest matters. The same with
the non-achievement, and the uttermost effort for it. Here I
see the humble mind; and the only sphere, ultimately, of
humility. . . . The *Staretz* is not without being chosen, willing or very unwilling, by the disciple; and freely chosen by a
compelling vision beyond the person, and chosen – if for life
– then only because the vision pulls; should it break down,

[1] cf. vii, March 24th, 1975 (p. 94)

there would be no breach, because the disciple rests *free* to choose, free forever, and to follow his own understanding of the initial vision.

February 11th, 1975
I have very much on my mind that the *minds* of monks must be fed.[1] The spirit grows with the mind. They must know why they are monks – inwardly – and why once a monk, one could never narrow oneself down to anything else. It is all a question of the comprehension of what love in its highest fulfilment is, and what it is not primarily. But then there will not be many, but why should there be many? It is glorious to pay all the cost.[2]

February 18th, 1975
So we cannot control the spirit; 'nothing' can in a moment become everything for one soul. And these moments count, whether the ship be sinking to the outward eyes or not. One should not perhaps allow the sinking image to gain upon one. If Christ is guiding the sinking it can never be one, but just a call of endurance to the end, which is real and a great thing. All the values are upside down in the monastic life and there are things that simply do not and will not apply.

February 26th, 1975
People come and love us because we are outwith society; and for nothing in the world would I lose being outside society in order to love more, not less. I cannot believe in a monastic life towards a set immanent end: although I can see that end achieved by the way, more painfully and certainly without apparent success.

March 18th, 1975
What I can ever and ever not understand is, how in practical stresses, a veil goes down over one's inner life, so that one cannot get through. In a way one *can* not pray. Last week this happened again till we reached the conclusion and by Sunday gained some peace. But this, one probably feels in an exagg-

[1] cf. VII, March 24th, 1975 (p. 94)
[2] cf. VI, July 24th, 1969 (p. 78)

erated way and perhaps the anguish of it *is* a form of prayer
we cannot recognize in ourselves. But that, to the last, I
should be so impressed is ridiculous. But look how the
'saints' funked administration in all ages and left it to others. I
simply can not do both. I erupted into a desperate lamenta-
tion about it and in the end realized that I was only part of a
huge family of monks who had precisely the same – and
perhaps the same words even for it. I believe one must stop
getting impressed over oneself and take it as a positive work –
to endure this total eclipse under stress – and now the building years. I wonder how many monks cursed the cathedral
building, the noise of hammering and the worries and endless
accidents. So they revenged themselves with the gargoyles
and devils to show what they thought of it!!

June 2nd, 1975 [from Cookridge Hospital]
The Matron resolved to give me a holiday and put me into a
room to myself overlooking the hills and Leeds at the end of a
large ward of four bays. And – for a check-up – ... I took
with me the *Brothers Karamasov*, which led my youth first
into nursing and then into the Orthodox Church. So I go
back forty to fifty years and see how the roots have power,
and what a Russian idealist, as Dostoievsky despite of all was,
expected of a *Staretz* – and on the first page I read I found the
heresy of the absolute power of the *Staretz* on earth and in
heaven! Not the Ecumenical Patriarch can absolve the monk
from the simple command of the *Staretz*. So I shall have fun
and labour in justifying my own course of non-direction.

June 6th, 1975
And it seems to me that only the truly homeless can be, and
are, home for the other because they do not form hedges
around their earthmade cherished 'home'. So any homeless
tramp feels at ease with us and in 'his own', from whatever
station he may be, professor, hotel-keeper, or vagrant. There
are no limits, of whatsoever religion or non-religion. My
childhood's dream has ever been: all, and no fences, no frontiers, no exclusions. And a tiny bit of that, in as far as it is
possible, our tiny Monastery may mean for some who recognize the spirit of it. But here there came a sad conflict with

the Greeks, who would have taken us over wholesale, and, of course, poured money into the Monastery *if* we would only follow *them*. The glory of this earth was laid before me by a 'multi-millionaire' who wished to found a monastery (and rule it!), and after a fight of one or two hours with me, his friend said: 'You see, for Mother Maria it is not a question of money!' So we travelled North. The invasion (literally) would have caught us up soon in the London orbit. Here we are now, poor, but with land to cultivate, forgotten of London, with the highest monastic dignity, equipped by the Archbishop[1] (it was a lovely service), following blindly the Spirit's promptings inside, through many hazards. But we have now an English priest,[2] Orthodox, who will visit us every two to three months, a lecturer at Oxford, and in our Jurisdiction; he discovered us at long last, inwardly, and so all can be well from that point of view.

June 10th, 1975
Somebody brought me Merton's selection of the wisdom (*Verba Patrum*) of the desert, and, to my infinite delight, the selection hit almost every characteristic of our own mad monastic life in essence! I was much comforted. We always meant to be that – and the 'not judging' was at the core, as with us; and the total lack of superimposition of outward form; and the mockery over piousity.[3]

June 29th, 1975
Even in my slenderest part, monastic superiority[4] is a terrible killer. Something must be wrong, or perhaps not, perhaps we are meant to be slain. I am longing for wider horizons and better sight. This rambling about in total darkness is no small task. But the temerity in resisting the society-world at least makes Gospel sense, and the Gospel becomes one's only home. I have such a happiness inside me, and I *want* to be happy in the face of any devil.

[1] the bestowal of the Great Schema on Mother Maria
[2] Father Kallistos
[3] an adapted word frequently used by Mother Maria to emphasize an active piousness aimed at effect, rather than a simple condition
[4] a reference to being an Abbess, even with so small a monastery

Christmas 1975
Yet I cannot doubt of a mathematically precise guidance, in
which I believe; and the one and only task of monks I can see
is to open the heart wide, as if it were heaven – in a faith that
will not acknowledge boundaries; and then see what happens. Patterns, even non-patterns will not carry us through.
Fanfares are necessary where numbers increase. And numbers are really only needed where a set work is taken up to be
'materially' accomplished, but perhaps even more in order to
carry the weaker who need company. But a few may have to
endure barrenness to the uttermost.

[No date] 1976
I believe that it is the witness of the monk to the eternal, to
preach the tenderness of God, and to live it, and the living I
see in transfiguring inside the heart the meanest attempt of
love, of others, or the smallest radiation of light, into glory.
See them all as glory, even if they will stick to earthly splendour. I only now see something of how men hide themselves
assiduously before one another, in order not to be slain.
Perhaps this is a necessity, but I just wonder, what would
happen, if that chain of fear were broken asunder; I see something like the eruption of Etna. The force of it might carry
the other along. Fear is of the devil. And why not be slain? It
is remarkable, how one can get happily used to it, and the one
enemy are not the slayers, but the fear of losing the faith. But
the faith grows in defeating the fear. The enemy of the monk
is the everlasting fear for protecting one's 'spiritual life'. 'The
cause, the cause!' The more we try, the less God has space to
protect it. One must let go fear and step out into the darkness
of the cruelty of men. And remember that nothing is more
cruel than children can be; and perhaps a cruel man is but a
child who wants to be loved and guided, to get the bitterness
unfrozen in him. I once heard an Indian bishop say: 'If we are
to be crucified, so, let us be crucified.'

February 7th, 1976
I am alone, thinking how right the Rechabites were. There is
something queer in building houses, stifling the spirit. The
mere fact of building draws the spirit continually away from
where it wants to abide. So equally I am continually rushing

and stretching back, mostly just patiently – or not – in the dark.

March 24th, 1976[1]
But we must admit that in our piecemeal world fighters *are* needed, and the work is divided. The monk has the liberty to go into the non-fighting camp, and this is his privilege, but he may also be a fighter, as many were. Only in the non-fighting the Gospel comes very near, and a creative participation in 'following' the realization of perfect love on earth.

April 17th, 1976
I have always understood monastic obedience as the training *par excellence* of transcending the middle sphere by being called incessantly towards the *causa finalis*, and the claim to obedience only showing the irrelevance of the middle sphere – and the demand to consent to it. For the commands are more often than not objectively stupid. It was arrant stupidity to waste my time and strength at sewing in the Abbey if I took it in that sense. The monk must, however, put the sense into it himself; to put the reality beyond the visible world and the way to it through the self-transcendence, with no regret. 'Nature' in the Platonic tradition can, and often does, mean the primal image of God, towards which we are striving to fulfil it. And this makes eminent sense. But on earth we never get beyond the 'between', and that which is mixed; and the striving is best done by keeping the eyes fixed on heaven.

September 29th, 1976
I often wondered what it meant when I saw myself restricted outwardly into a set form; though this sat ever lightly on me. I wondered if it could only be done inwardly, but the vision ever recurred as a guiding voice. There are three images for it and none of them coincided with my Monastery, though I knew them to be my innermost, my very own life: though I also knew the Monastery not to be a sideline, nor a détour. The three mental images, very real, came at the outset of my monastic life when I was in the whirlwind of a definite unquestioned vocation, and thought it would be a hidden, secular monastic life. I first, for a year, did not mean to enter a monastery. I then saw myself as a big, square, rough old

[1] cf. II, May 25th, 1970 (p. 18)

house; there was no glass in the windows, all very poor. But a lamp burning night and day for anyone who would come for a night or longer into one of the rooms – not to me. I would hardly know who was there. If they would remain unknown I would let them; I was just the house, a place of welcome and warmth and infinite compassion (in the true sense) – being one with each inwardly, demanding nothing, teaching nothing – above all no judging or categories or piousity of any kind, but the light every night showing the way.

The second very forceful image of the same time, I saw during the funeral of an uncle at Bern. I do yet not know what it meant, but it remained the same ever since in force; and I often wonder if it pointed beyond death. There was in the cemetery chapel a bare, huge, brick wall, and there I saw myself in the form of a tall way-mark, just a sign, totally still, disconnected but relevant, showing into one direction, sideways (to heaven); and below at my feet an infinite torment of a mass of suffering people, distorted, with no unity, just names of terror, worse than wars or anything imaginable: I was not part of it except by the direction. They were past any human help, nor was I human. There was just that tall, total stillness; of suffering – also perhaps the expectation of the end of it. I was at the time completely absorbed and I often returned to it. When I went into the Abbey I had an idea of the Monastery, a one-roomed, poor hut on a hill, again an open door and people coming and going, again a shelter. I always saw Filgrave like it.

February 26th, 1977
Having cut off all the fringes, I still see a monk in the image of the open road into the transcendent world, and being in a way a 'general' person accessible to all and outside conventional boundaries and cares for society with all the lies of it.[1]

May 15th, 1977 (G)
In the *Philokalia* there is a comforting saying of a *Staretz*, that when all goes well, one must be on one's guard. There could be something wrong somewhere. If that is the norm, we are certainly on a safe path.

[1] cf. vii, December 29th, 1974 (p. 92); and x, December 12th, 1974 (pp. 139ff)

VI DYING TO THE WORLD

*Passivity – living – unifying of will – worldly
success – values – judgement – teaching*

The *dying to the world* in his out-of-society life may be easier
for the monk, but far from his exclusive right. It is open to all
who are ready to suffer the non-solution, to pray without an
immanent end, to throw away the passivity of living rela-
tively to demands from outside. The *dying to the world* is the
glad paradox of the Christian life: to die that we might live.
And to live a life to Christ means the effort of drawing the
will out of the multiplicity of so-called free will to the one
transcendent end: and hence follows the inattention to success, as far as the world is concerned, but unceasing work at
whatever we do in the knowledge that our work will be
judged not by worldly, but by heavenly measures. We live
inside the Mystery of the Judgement, and the value of what
we do, as the Parables teach us, we cannot gauge. So we may
not judge, not only others but ourselves; yet we must work
while it is still day. So, in the light of the Mystery, 'absolute'
teaching becomes distasteful, if not well-nigh impossible,
and demand for 'absolute' direction a wrong and false humility. Obedience should be sovereign, in the consent of the
mind, facing only towards the *incomprehensible* Truth.

[No date] *1952*
And wherever in life there is work which *is* not rest, then
beware! hell is near. *How* much hell and mental sickness are
the same! Where a person breaks up into a plurality – and so
never finds rest again. . . .[1] We shall be all right – because we

[1] cf. v, April 11th, 1968 (p. 62)

shall be in heaven soon. That is our only comfort, because comfort there is none on earth, for those who do not believe in success.... I saw that one step towards humility could be to accept Christ's humility, that he does not refuse to dwell in the most wicked soul. That would mean that I let go *all* my own prognosis for anything and to leave all room to the wonders of God, and to *utter hope* for anyone. And as soon as I see a hopelessness, I shall know that I see shadows, which God does not see in myself or in others. And that pride is *to stick to one's own judgement, without taking into account God's transforming creative love.*

March 26th, 1952
I also saw the reason of those parables of judgement, which have to be spoken against the 'double ignorance'. The frightful shock, 'I know you not', is the last, the utter limit of Love's call, God tearing his own heart to pieces. How could he not know, calling as he did? But the operation might be needed. This sentence: 'I know you not' can never be uttered by us, for then it would have a different and ungodly meaning. In this the Church has often gone astray. There are things which must be exclusively left to God. No wonder he gave such severe warning against 'judging a brother'. He warns us that the judgement is entirely his; that last desperate call of Love he reserves for himself alone.

October 9th, 1952
If 'to forgive' means to accept God's forgiving – and nothing less – then it means a lot. Reproach for one's own sins is easy and fruitful, but extremely difficult to bear reproach against others – and *there* was the loneliness, to keep faithful to the good I saw in their evil-doing, and for the evil, faithful to God's forgiveness without restriction. It is easy to apply the codex of deadly sins, but a question if it is the way *God* sees things. All depends on *how* things were done.

January 4th, 1953
One could ... take with a kind of inner delight the occasions on which we can grow – everything which happens on the bridge. One has nearly found the treasure, hidden, when one

does, once for all, no more try to find some easier and better outward circumstances, but take the things as the material, the notes and syllables for a song, sung for God with all the heart and tenderness and great expectancy. I love so much, and have never enough of the first chapter of I Peter, that day, when *the* great hope was born in us. And the tribulations if they are necessary ... (never a bit more than what is necessarily used and needed by God) to make shine forth the faith, lovelier than silver or gold. It can all be used, all can be loved, and about everything the heart can rejoice; because in every darkness or sorrow or fear it can still secretly say to God, 'Look, I love you' and he must look at once, and he loves our tiny little tests of trust. And as soon as one gets a glimpse of the joy of God's heart, then all turns into glory at once; it never leaves us again quite. Therefore, I think, there are nothings of little importance; our personal affairs; they can shoot up into eternity any minute and we *have* no other means of showing God our love, than in our own petty affairs; they are, as such, never small. Is it perhaps a small thing to plant in a child a garden of love for God and men? or lovingly to return roughness and insult by gentleness? It is easy to fall in and take it as small, but the smallest event becomes wider than the wide world, when God is in it. I am deeply convinced that the outward solutions come about by themselves and with certainty, when one comes to accept fully that in which one is.

November 6th, 1954
All judging, or aversion, all human reactions must die and only love remain. But it must be active love, love which can love on their own level, love them as they are. Charles de Foucauld's Order and the priest-workmen have found the point at which Christians *can* meet communism.

July 5th, 1961
The world simply does not interest me any more, except in that sense which does not interest the world. So we constantly miss.

August 1965
The faculty of free will: not man's glory but a symptom of

weakness, the broken, divided will. Intending finite things determines the will by the immanence of the object; only a transcendent end unifies the will, and in its unification lies the freedom and expansion of all the faculties. Here lies the centre in thought of monastic obedience. But the freedom can be attained whenever a finite end is intended for the one transcendent end. In other words, freedom is love, and in love we are able to transcend the frontiers of reason, which must move inside contradictory ideas.

October 8th, 1965
The evidence grows inside me day by day, as if it were something done; I mean something which God has already accomplished and the working of it out in time, which he gives us to do, is something like copying his own work: by looking and looking at him. It is *so* difficult to concentrate on earth when heaven is so near. It is almost impossible; and the most austere training of self-transcendence; as long as it is absolutely needed.

February 3rd, 1966
I refuse to acknowledge important things to exist versus unimportant ones *within* the immediate realm of duty – and without *total* concentration nothing worthwhile is *ever* achieved. It is not a sermon, but something which is terribly important to me. I am incapable of acting in anything except out of a full recollection.

June 20th, 1967
It is so comforting that we need no 'success'. We just *are* and have no plans nor any immanent ends. This, most of all, confuses hierarchs, I believe. And I am not very merciful and like to hide that which really matters to me.

December 27th, 1967
We make our way day by day, creeping along, or hurrying or flying, it all comes to the same ultimately, and one day it will all go into insignificance, worked and woven into the present of heaven, wholly.

January 22nd, 1968

Meeting Christ personally [Fr Lev's book on the Parables] is the real concern, seeing the shining face of Christ, being gripped by him. The immediacy of evidence. I find this direct form of teaching very hard to take, yet people live on it. It is an easier course where one can still talk and think that talking will help. But there is a point where words cease and where we will not entrust our lives to them, or rather our faith, because it becomes impossible – it is no longer within the outwardness of the being a thing thought about, but it has become ourselves.

February 7th, 1968

'Presence' is by far the loveliest task; millions of miles above teaching; I think. Forgive me, it is my battlehorse.

[The following extracts were written to Sister Katherine between April 11th, 1968 and July 24th, 1969.]

... Perhaps hell could be trying to live earthly limitations (if worshipped as perfection) 'eternally' and never achieving it, like Sisyphus or Tantalus.

... and that is what I always desired, to make others think on their own.

... Gauss once said that the ultimate perfection on earth, the summit of a philosopher's life, is when he lays down his office, and in utter self-transcendence is only an adviser to the young, in full respect, giving them the possibility of freedom to go astray. In this attitude one can see precisely the force which will hold them from not going astray! the enthusiasm of following a non-threatening and non-forcing call.

... If the initial evidence is there, it carries one through every trial. But if one started on a course of human decision and human 'kindness', one would have to carry it through with one's own strength, and one's own plans, and there would be a very long way to catch up God's plan anew. What looks like ascent is so often a descent and I felt this danger so acutely ... and there is always this shattering seeming evidence on the worldly level.

... People always think success has to do with numbers. But Christ thought twelve were enough for him. And how

often did Gauss insist that it could only be the few.[1]
... I came across that lovely bit where Plato (Gauss) traces
the ages, how the ascent never stops, and when retired from
work (at sixty with Plato, or even earlier) the last epoch
begins, with no more active work, but only advising, and
this is the most austere: to give to the young the freedom of
going astray, without imposition of will. And this will go on
till death. There is no decay in a life lived towards the *causa
finalis*, no break in the ascent, and no release of increasingly
heavier demands.

November 17th, 1969
The mirrors are marred – only death is true – only in death
am I seeable – or that moment before death – when the world
is a dream.

July 15th, 1970
I must be allowed to work behind someone's back. When I
can, as it were, feed one mind, who then refashions it to give
it out; then I can write; but I can't do the direct teaching. And
I do not think that this is only shyness. It is an inner 'No'. I
tried to break through it by the publishing efforts, and only
found my instincts confirmed. The moment I step out of my
frame, the one thing I can give is lost, and gets blurred within
the network of alien adjustments at once demanded, and so I
lose my own ground. But I will *gladly* have the girl here, if
she likes to come, or *anyone* who wishes to come. It is an
everlasting mystery to me, but perhaps now the pattern will
arise more clearly.

September 28th, 1970
... and not a scrap of teaching or wanting to teach is left; I
cannot help it. I don't want to teach. But I *so* want to make
people see, feel and rejoice in that they *are* inside the Truth
and *can* not fall out of it.

December 12th, 1973
The measure, we measure, and how we understand the Truth
of God, will be checked by higher measures which we do not

[1] cf. v, February 11th, 1975 (p. 67)

know and of which the parables constantly remind us. There will be surprises.

June 28th, 1974
More and more, I know, that to be a treasure-store of comfort, a descent into hell in our small measures, somehow, somewhere, is needed; to have marched to the brink – of human possibility of endurance, and relentless torments of 'futility' in one's work; to take this up – as a work – and the result comes unexpectedly, from a completely different side.

December 29th, 1974
Let's crawl along on all fours, only let's not be strong ever. That I should fear.... Sometimes it seems as if, on the road described, faith turned into vision. No longer is it a salvation ever from outside, but an inward-working principle of every minute, though, of course, in the constant sense of total inadequacy – *measured with that* which is not mixed, and this of course is the spur onwards; the field of work is endless and urgent and present.

February 16th, 1975
I was terribly sorry to hear of your disappointment over the manuscript; mercifully values are changing the nearer death comes, and it is the effort and love given to it which counts in the spiritual realm and which there remains as a reality active, I always believe. So there is nothing for tears in worldly non-success.

February 16th, 1975
I feel that once the decision is reached, you should make it *your own*, and not be passive towards it. Take it up and work with it. We get into a weak position if we fly into being coerced from outside; and then resent. Shake off resentment. Outward circumstances can never determine the soul, if the soul is alert and ready.

March 1975
I used to play the violin and it was like coming into another life of mine to hear the violin again; my first experience of the

transcendent in early life. I never played terribly well, but assiduously, and inwardly with ever greater longing to play better. So my non-achievement in the transcendent had its roots very deep and early. It mattered nothing. We can only 'attend' with love, it is enough, and long for the perfect to come.

March 11th, 1975
I just sometimes sense one danger, that is of a too speedy and zealous attempt of respectable 'definition' of the 'work'. It should not be too quick – and should perhaps never be; or only as a compromise.

May 15th, 1975
The whole difference, even friends did not always see, was the austerity of the determination of paying any cost and that the goal always remained transcendent to me in the strictest sense, and the demands severe. This is inherent in regarding all that *is*, all that matters ultimately, as *work*, and not earthly work as work, and I believe here comes the perspective and proportion of non-achievement, where it makes more sense. Perhaps a little transfiguringly and forgetting all the nonsense attached to it, one might refer to St Paul's idea that what is not done by faith is nothing. . . . Another aspect is praying for 'rest' eternal; it precisely fits. As we have no better words. Work as being is rest. Rest is just Being; but also 'their works follow them'. I like Taylor's idea, of taking that as meaning the heavenly works. They are not 'done'. And if one puts it into one's head to lead on earth a life – in 'heavenly measures' as far as possible – it again fits to try to 'be' prayer, or at least to make that the goal; and by happily swimming in love's ocean, to make that one's work (without leaving aside the gymnasium of the petty piecemeal work laid upon us) – but there can never be success within this frame of life. I see in the acceptance of this the genuineness of the other: the test. I found myself almost universally misapprehended by non-achievement – which, of course, is only towards the eternal measures.[1]

---

[1] cf. III, May 3rd, 1977 (p. 41) and March 24th, 1976 (p. 82)

June 2nd, 1975

I know, I take the non-direction to its uttermost limit. But only so, I believe, a true transference is possible. If one goes right down to the bottom of it, I wonder if the demand for direct direction is not every time a trial of excluding suffering. To find a highway, on which safely to travel to heaven and round the terrible perplexities.

June 6th, 1975

Don't grieve too much over the refusal, there is no significance in it, which would carry beyond death. And, who knows, perhaps this last blow you would not miss for anything when you arrived on the shore, and a long, hard life is being telescoped into one ray of glory and will grow into more and more glory. We have our beginning to come. And the older we get, the younger we are, in relation to heaven, for the stretch becomes smaller – and then we shall properly and finally *begin* to live. Try to be happy (or not-happy) – (I often am not), but we are looking forward.

August 12th, 1975

I ever only wanted to hint at a possible direction of thought, not more; to leave full freedom to each. And also I did never really know the Canons till now – the last minute to get to heaven with them.

First Monday of Lent, 1976

I am very quiet, can see only failure and mistake upon mistake, though even that matters nothing; but still very quietly my heart expands, knowing that now I would not have the physical strength to endure that joy of these strange days, so full of radiance not of this world. And now in our solitude I sometimes long for people. I always loved people. But even there I have hardly the strength. I remembered a refrain of the Bohemian Brothers which I now constantly pray, 'Thanks to you, ever and ever, Jesus Christ, that you are the sinful world's Saviour, that death and hell you have conquered,' and it seems to shed light over me that in the end all *is* praise and thanks ever and ever. As if the heavy responsibility which oppresses me is really none at all, as nothing rests in my hands, and any mistake is easily turned round by God

into a not-mistake. But more and more deeply I do take the
illness now as my actual work for the last stretch.

March 24th, 1976
One could link what I call non-achievement with – in Cudworth's thinking – the impossibility for our finite reason to
attain to a criterion of Truth; this would mean that we could
place ourselves outside Truth and judge it like a possession.
But we are inside it, surrounded on all sides, unable – even in
hell – to fall out of it; only inside ourselves we can be 'out'
and unaware. And the non-achievement, in *every* field, is that
we cannot grasp it even adequately, either in mind or in will;[1]
and this is at the same time our lifelong work – working in
the half not-seeing towards seeing more and more, and
extending our will wider and wider towards what we can
grasp of Truth; which again is a work stretching through life
into eternity. But Truth and Love are one; and so, in the
work of thinking we are also working to love and the other
way round, if we can get ourselves to purify our motives, not
placing the goal on a finite achievement as such, although the
work can only be done within our partial piecemeal field of
action and pseudo-achievement. So there always remains an
infinity of work awaiting and undone, and what we do is
firmly linked to what we shall do with our wider faculties in
heaven. So the non-achievement is the joy of the promise,
and the repentance already the participation in the future
work.

April 17th, 1976
I like to avoid the image of ascent which ever suggests the
Aristotelian ladder; opposed to the Platonic concept that the
most despicable thing is founded and held in the transcendence directly (i.e. Plato from *Parmenides* onwards where he
found the generalization of ideas). Therefore I like Cudworth's expression of extending the soul to the extent of the
will of God. One can understand this as an expansion to
integrate the most despicable thing, as God holds it all. 'Be
perfect', 'resist not evil'. That removes sin into a strangely
different orbit; and things get exciting. And because of the
'between' of our whole existence, repentance is the negative

---

[1] cf. May 15th, 1975 (p. 80)

achievement and the only true 'work', though it can only be done if the mixed work is also conscientiously done, as the training to which we are called. Without that we never come into the orbit of repentance, which is only towards God. Only God understands where we fail, often most deeply in our successes; yet we must work for these with all our might; and there lies the humility. Again, not towards men. Humility is a thing of mind foremost: the consent to the piecemeal work; and knowing that we never reach the goal, yet not to leave off or slacken. All this removes *all* our work deeply from the platform of human discussion or from dependence on others' behaviour, and there lies the ultimate freedom; although at the same time the whole work goes towards loving people, but that is only possible, if we do not – from the innermost – depend on them. The freedom as I see it is the orientation relentlessly and without mercy to oneself on to the transcendent world, which alone does not determine us, because in that way of life, life does not depend on any outward circumstances. In a way one could only find orientation to the transcendent sphere by dying to the middle sphere to a more and more vast extent. It is an absorbing task and I am still at it. We certainly have not achieved the exclusion of the middle sphere, but the work is yet going on in the stadium and this is perhaps more important than any show of perfection, which in many ways is far more comfortable than loving. Only – is there a lie in it? That is where I see 'the negative leadership'; by entering the contest in the stadium instead of from outside conducting the fight. But it is a hell of a life and we at present are certainly sitting in the nethermost hell. Cudworth said: 'God will not, and hell cannot, harm us,' a comforting word. In Romans 8, where all the dominions are counted up, one could read that positively, that no absorption in anything can separate us from God, because it is absorbed inside the love of God. That would make a clear end of the Protestant fear that the saints take away the prerogative of Christ and all that in very many disguises.[1] The saints again are in a sense our stadium; to widen our love towards the extent of the love of God, and let them all in till we burst. It is lovely to roam about freely in my 'country'.

[1] cf. I, July 12th, 1967 (p. 4)

June 23rd, 1977

I can see very clearly your question about parish work or (and) writing, and how weariness makes you *feel* slothful, perhaps more than you really are. I think the solution will gradually work itself out *from inside*. It is a very dear idea to me in the Orthodox ascetic tradition, that a monk after profession may go through a few years of great spiritual consolation, but then a darkness comes down and the endurance of emptiness is demanded; and to feel empty, inadequate, and not-seeing is, to my mind, a thing with which you *can* work safely and healthily, maybe through a lifetime, or most of it, if you keep your inner attention quite simply on learning to love. It is not possible to live your spiritual life continually on a high note. The Holy Spirit is a very tender Person, and tenderly leads us by the hand to learn to suffer a little, also suffer our failure, because then the greater mysteries will unfold themselves quietly in our soul. I remember a day when I made a lot of effort, and a priest told me that I must learn to rest in God. That idea of 'resting' came like an infinite release. God does not exact great exploits from us, he only desires us to love *and* to understand with our mind (I mean by mind something far more than simple reasoning on a worldly plane), what Christ means by love. Love is not in the first place a sentiment, but a definite work which gets more and more exciting, the further one goes; and then from there any 'activities' take on their true proportions, they are not so important.

July 14th, 1977

Judging others is an ugly thing, because it presupposes that we 'know' what God only knows, their innermost heart – and also that we know our own innermost heart, which we certainly do not. . . . Again in earthly cares and the Kingdom – they are on two levels and cannot be pitted against one another – the cares may persist, but we learn their unimportance (and much of it is irrelevant) the more we look up and forward to the Kingdom, and we learn to laugh at ourselves. With that the worst is already overcome, though we go on worrying. It is a question of priority of love.

VII THE WORK OF LOVE

*Integration of evil – reality of the person – the
centre*

If we remain firmly unmoved by any seeming success, if we
know we have failed before God and yet hold to the hem of
his garment, Saviour and Judge, then the work of love can
begin: the integration of evil: the carrying and redirecting
into the one transcendent aim. The work of love is to see the
reality in others, God within them, or, perhaps, as God created them out of Love. The integration of evil derives in the
first count from the effort of drawing all back into the innermost core, the centre within each of us, which holds the
Mystery of the Presence, however hidden and obscured by
every kind of distortion. The work of love is to see the centre
in others as their one reality, and then of loving the person in
his reality. This work is active and *personal*, never the imper-
sonal evasion of the nebulous 'loving God in others'. No, our
work is rather to love others in the one part which still rests
in God, and suffer all the fringes. Of course, this is not possible. Our feelings, our own middle sphere, all the compromise of life prevents the work. It must be a failure except for
the rarest occasions. But we can carry the failure, trusting
that Christ will himself fill in our gaps. It is in no wise
missionary work, far from any attempt at 'reform', it is simply the unattainable attempt to follow Christ in his love,
which carried the sins of the world as a whole. To redirect
evil, if only once in a lifetime, by non-reaction, is the seed of
the Kingdom of Heaven. The work cannot be popular, there
is nothing to show.

[No date] 1951

We must not 'sit down' and rest before we have widened our hearts *so* much as to consider every life and the most disgraceful one, with tender *receiving* all of it. And when we are not yet able, there it remains the humble acknowledgement of our finite capacity and vision and the pain and blame is on us; because we never know whether, if we could receive it, we might not turn it round: and so the debts are without number, always; and these debts of love are our very safeguard, because they hurry us to fly right into the heart of God, where there are no such limitations of love as in us. And there we have nothing else to do than to delight in his love – i.e. the final victory over any kind of holy jealousy.

[No date] 1952

... so far as death is achieved in life, so far only can death be seen as reality, and hope grows – it is a mystery for those who refuse death, and remains a source of doubt for them; another aspect of, that only as far as we love, we understand love and know God – *and* have hope of resurrection. The hope at once turns into doubt when we do not actually live love, i.e. *actually* die. This attitude of the love of dying in order to know God, and grow into Love, actively, lovingly, *joyfully* – is humility; it is our fashion of perfection, as long as the only realization of love is turning evil into good, humility is the loving of the enemy, really, actually, by no means only as an object of pity – but the acute pain of refusal of love.

[No date] 1952

There is even for us an omnipotence in love. What evil can meet us which love cannot bear? One can break under it – but that does not sweep love's power away; and there is the tremendous comfort that, in breaking down, love's work is not hindered. I think there is no possible greater comfort in the whole world than being allowed, comfortably, to break down and be killed. What can they do? Only kill the body – what does that mean to God? There is really no limit put for love in the world – there is no victory against love from no side.

[No date] 1952
Joy is the trick of turning evil; and dis-evil[ing] it. There
seems somehow no hell before me without heaven. That [has
been] done already somehow. And as my vocation is joy, the
point in it *is* the seeing of heaven and having it as the only
reality; and none beside it. Joy implies the *entire* selflessness;
and it is important that even chance is dis-eviled and all
weight taken off even of martyrdom; because in joy it
became natural. There is no higher goal on earth than the
making of selflessness *natural*; and one essence; and taking self
as real only in the specific vision of heaven.

March 26th, 1952
I always feel an uneasy mistake in that attitude of 'Christian
loyalty' towards a big mistake which can be seen. There is
something of untruth in it; it is like gunpowder, ready to
explode on the first occasion, not a transforming creative
power. Love must go further; beyond all human possibilities
of generosity and self-discipline, which again and again
shows me its dangerous face. And this going beyond is *not*
asked of all. There is no abyss, no inward or outward divi-
sion, which love cannot heal. No outward victory is to be
expected, but, as it were, a steady, unseen, from-moment-
to-moment restoring of the wounds and ever-new breaches
of this spiritual union. 'Loyalty' makes things too harmless
on one side, and on the other deepens the breach.

October 1953
The heart must love and forgive where there is little to love
and much to forgive, and must love in the transport of that
divine superabundance of love – simply for love's sake,
regardless of worth, or right use, or anything whatsoever.
The fruits come slowly, but surely, and there is no other
victory over evil.

July 1955
I see that the contemplative way of converting souls is to hold
fast to the vision of their souls in the heart of God, and to let
that work by itself. It is seeing the tracks of glory, the solitary

sunbeams in heathen souls, and leaving aside the rest and not
trying to convert it.

[No date] 1959
It is a bit like out on the sea; one never knows when a wind-
blast comes again; but the more there are which have passed
without damage, the more composedly one takes the next
one. The thing is, I think, to take them *naturally*, as it were,
with the least inner effort. I mean the kind of effort which
wears one out. I think it is a very important thing to establish
regular Confession and Communion, so that it becomes a
thing that is natural and not a 'shall I, or shall I not?' It does
feed the soul and stabilizes an inner pool of peace in the soul,
a *réduit* and a strength which less and less fears the storms, or
better, turns the storms into so many blessings.

July 1961
The only thing we can give one another in life is the 'raw
material' of love and of sacrifice; then the other must build
for himself. When the material is good, the building will
stand firm and beautiful. Divine love is always non-
protective, and it is not hard to accept it, though it hurts.

September 1965
Love can never be anything else but personal. In speaking of
not being able to take another's suffering away, I meant that
this is the greatest pain, a sort of crucifixion, the deepest
austerity we can reach or suffer. Never would I consider a
sort of general love which speaks lightly of suffering; nor of a
submission to the divided will. It is the heart's joy, and I can
only think of taking it up actively and creatively, at all costs,
and making it my own. The price will always be high – but
do we want a cheap life?

November 17th, 1967
It is never a short cut to clear obstacles away; the way is
shortest through the obstacles: clearing them away they are
also out of control, and at unexpected times and places come
walking in again when time is less favourable because the
divine plan is disturbed.

December 1974
From this vision and life of love it is very strange how people react if they are met with a living and warm love which demands nothing in return. The fearlessness towards convention is a formidable weapon of love, but it may only be used if the middle sphere is *dead-alive* or alive in death, if the centre itself has swallowed it up in the irresistible gravitation, although it still fully lives. Here I see the Gospel depart from all eastern religions and of course from every effort of gaining power in any sphere.

December 4th, 1974
I see the monk's freedom to love in the integration of the whole of the 'middle sphere' into the openness of the 'centre' – but what that means! It is nothing less than the renunciation of every human *claim* of fulfilment, in the sense, feeling, thinking (in a sense), but at the same time being warm, alive (not deadened), embracing without the claim of holding; and wholly without fear.

It is in the 'middle sphere', and not in the 'centre' – where the traps of intimacy lie for the monk; although even that can lead forward, if it is suffered well. I find this always for myself, important. The innermost is not the intimate, exclusive, to-be-sheltered sanctuary, but a wide open land, where *all* are meant.

December 6th, 1974
When I stopped I meant to say that the monk's innermost centre is a land where all are allowed in, invited in, with heavy boots or delicate steps, ravaging or tender. And never mind what the middle sphere feels, plans (in triumph of planning or planning despair); our work lies in 'not-resisting evil' – which only means, 'be ye perfect'. When I was thirty-five, after reading a philosophical work of Gauss, I was suddenly seized with such a vision of love, that I could hardly bear the joy of it. For weeks I walked as in a trance; I dug into the NT and all of a sudden every word made sense, and every contradiction sense also. From then on it was merely a matter of expression and of living it forward. The immediate result, written in ecstasy, was *Evil in the New Testament*.

Then I saw love as something far beyond the middle-sphere love, but *not* disconnected from it. In the disconnection (non-attachment) I see so much of the monastic blunder of fear, and of a dead death. It is the vision that the highest fulfilment of love – any love – but always love of a person, is in the turning of evil into good, for love. Taking the evil (or doubt) into the heart and there secretly turning it all into gold by refusing to give power, force, or 'person' to evil. But then I saw how Christ did it wholly, and how he calls us to follow in that particular work, precise, and here lies, in full, the reverting of every form of passivity into a creative grasp; in Christ – even of death. Love burns with a sovereign flame.

But again, it is not possible to do it, or to begin, by thinking one could ever achieve it. I began on one tiny but deeply relevant sphere.

December 29th, 1974
Then suddenly stands before one the claim to grow up; as if a gigantic cross struck one in the innermost being. It seems incomprehensible darkness – but it is light. I know it is. It will be, and demands to be, believed as Light, blindly, consistently, as a fool. And from that infinitesimal point reality streams in and the centre opens wide and is home for all, and the Life begins in wide and great measure; because to turn darkness round *once*, where it hurts most, gives us a key to smaller occasions, and from that the whole Gospel only begins to make sense – and more and more sense, and active following. . . .

I want to talk a little more, and I tried to find precisely what I mean by 'tender integration'. I found that the only way of opening up the middle sphere into the transcendent innermost core is to make the senses (in the widest sense) love the spirit; and to follow it 'excitedly', even to their death, through their own being hurt all the time; and crying and ever suffering more. But the spirit also must love the senses, to get them going, and inspire them with beauty and vision.

But there must be somewhere a point of departure; and for this point each one, I believe, must wait, and it *is* a mystery when it comes, and terrible to endure. But there is, or can be, a grace in it – as of one tiny spark – of a *voluntary* death of the senses into the spirit – and if that threshold is presented to us and accepted as the highest grace that God gives – then the whole world changes its aspect. What seemed evil turns into good inside our heart, and the sorrow into joy inside the tears. Both together. The middle sphere goes on blundering happily, but no longer as an edifice – *there* I have the 'child' – never built upon, but tenderly led into 'growing to the fulness of the stature of Christ'. To the middle sphere, in a sense, and to this specific opening of it, also belong the Office and explicit prayer – how tenderly the Church is taking the senses by the hand ever and ever in patience.

But it really does become exciting, as soon as one discovers that it works, and that a radiance goes out, in the face of which evil loses threat and significance. But the beginning is a crucifixion in the heart; and the whole NT is full of it, once the clue is found. Only that threshold which is the mystery cannot be construed; so we can never judge where God 'punishes' or 'humiliates', far more probably he gives the 'grace of the mystery'. And, in time, once begun, one gets accustomed to see through the 'evil' and to bring it 'into the operation of the end'; and this is turning it into good.

And doing the same backwards, too. *But* we never reach the unmarred core purely – just because we may not leave the middle sphere behind, but have to work with it *inside* the open land, undoing cramps and accepting a thousand deaths; but since it all happens within the open centre, we cannot fall out of heaven, not with any amount of not-being-able-to-pray. Prayer is only the way, the worming through to the centre. Once there, we just *are*.

And the life of the monk, in his privilege of being less embroiled in the middle sphere, on all levels, social, etc. as well as personal, I see as *one* single witness to the open centre, and the opening the possible free access, and in our time, when the transcendence is either lost to sight, denied, *or* once again overlaid with pentecostal middle spheres, leading to new exclusion and non-freedom, I would choose nothing more dearly than this; and see no higher fulfilment than here, at the very workshop of life and death; including hell and heaven in one; darkness and light.

Also, when I speak of the encounter – alone – with Christ

at the End-point, I speak at the same time of the infinite
Communion of Saints ever with us, but one cannot say
everything in the same breath ... I understand the aloneness
and Communion ever as one.[1]

[No date] 1975 (G)
But I am wholly lost in the consciousness of political over-
responsibility, *everything* comes to me from another point of
view, and I cannot at all lament so ardently the world and its
ruin, and take it so seriously. Here, we in the Eastern Church
take it more lightly. We count with mistakes and know and
believe that mistakes will be put right in heaven, and not so
much responsibility lies on us as long as we love. But love
from all our soul, and love in all directions, and in an inex-
haustible joy, and leave it to others to decide what love is
worth or not.

January 4th, 1975
It is in the end only an inner homelessness[2] that we can offer
each other as home; and which releases the soul into flight; it
comes to the same as poverty; but I say 'inner'; it can so easily
revert into its contrary; and will, if and in as far as it is not the
open core, the vast land inside, opening to heaven. The
innermost openness is both homelessness and poverty – the
beatitudes are there, and the defence against any form of
subtle idealism in the sound of it.

January 14th, 1975 [a visit of Fr. John, o.d.c., with his young
friars]
The Carmelite youngsters (ordinands) were so refreshing.
Like sardines we sat round the kitchen table, on anything,
unable to move. I decided to do an Ahab – wounded on the
war chariot – and got through famously. Then one whis-
pered to Sister Katherine: 'The Lord will give her strength.' I
found it a lovely experience – in pre-death so wholly open 'to
see' and immediately, infinitely and with no bounds to love
other spirits, souls, persons with no barrier and no frontier
between – and Church and religion, any non-religion – but

[1] cf. i, June 4th, 1972 (p. 5) and viii, December 8th, 1973 (p. 105)
[2] cf. v, October 16th, 1965 (p. 60)

people. It is a glory to be allowed into the monastic freedom, where the poor bishops may never get on earth, in their confined shepherd limitation. We may rush ahead with the greater Shepherd and embrace the world; firmly anchored, anchored in divine and human love. I feel nothing except that I want to be happy in the great monk-family where I 'saw' myself introduced at my first vows in 1950. I then saw an immense multitude and warm welcome into a world-wide collection of monks across all the heavens and earth and relig-ions, and rejoiced to bursting point at the freedom and love-liness of it. And soon I shall be there and make it all the more and more sovereignly real to you.

March 11th, 1975
I thought, how precise it is that 'we shall know as we are known' (and what a perspective!) but St Paul never dared to say that 'we shall love as we are loved'. It will ever be more than what we can answer. And on earth, it is the only reason-able thing to do in view of what is coming and where we are going.

March 17th, 1975
Oh – let us at last have the faith released into freedom of movement of thought, and of love; unfraid and without defences – how it then could blossom!

March 24th, 1975
And I woke up with an exciting thought, how precisely the freedom of the land within can be lived on earth. It goes in two measures. First one begins in a very limited, and austerely and humbly limited, and consciously limited, way – trying out heavenly measures on a square inch of earth – and then, it grows quickly in one, no one noticing it, and, most importantly, without any effort of 'virtue', or forcing or wanting to achieve it, but one day one wakes up, rubs one's eyes and sees that, behind one's back the square inch has widened and a strange universalization has taken place, expanding more and more. (In a different context it is the widening from the first to the third diagram).[1] I was twenty-

---

[1] *The Realism of the Orthodox Faith*

four when I first took that course, where it hurt most, and
stuck to it. So it is now easy, and it was *blessing*. The more
difficult thing is the reverse course. But that is infinitely exciting, because it is wholly creative; but very subtle and requires
of course (or at least demands), the total integrity, but not in
a 'moral' setting. I just now realize that it is this precisely,
what I mean by the impetus which makes the senses *gladly* to
follow the spirit, and the whole middle sphere with no
reserve plunge into the gravitation of the open centre. The
first part is the negating of any flicker of passivity in the faith,
no resignation-comfort, but a voluntary going forward – but
also, in the Gospel, the ever demanded expanding of love
from the love and faith to God – to the love and faith to men.
Or rather, both as the same One. To do that wholesale makes
the freedom grow to such an extent that it takes one's breath
away; because nothing can constrain it, because it rests inside
the immediate traffic into the transcendence. I only this
morning got the reverse course, which I happily practised
very unconcerned as you know, so clearly in its significance.
But this, of course, can already not be taught, because it is a
mountain ridge, and presupposes the total willingness to suffer – gladly and unconcerned. The first step swiftly includes
the stepping out of passivity in any situation; and the second
step is really the same towards oneself. It is great fun to read
St Paul in his various circles of soundness or adaptation.
When he does not adapt, he says: 'I do not judge myself.' To
learn to love so, is, I think, the only definite work of the
monk, and the only, very only, reason for wanting to be one.
But also, once one sees it greatly, one could never want to be
anything else. It demands the whole person, and especially
the *mind*. The mind must be trained to the integrity of humility. The heart will follow the mind. It will have no choice.[1]

It is also in this context, and never in the moral middle-
sphere plane of responsibility (in the immanent sense) that
repentance belongs; which ever includes, inside the freedom,
the total inadequacy apart from the accidental failings ... it
so releasingly struck me, to what degree *all* evil is integrated
into the freedom of heaven. Evil literally carried as one whole

---

[1] cf. v, [no date] 1975 (p. 66) and v, February 11th, 1975 (p. 67)

(as I 'saw' it for the first time when I 'saw' and wrote *The Hidden Treasure*), and ever carried. And inside this realm, and because of it, dwelling upon our failings, in a way, denies that carrying from which springs our life, and which was from eternity. In a way God loves us so. He also (turning it round inside himself) sees whatever we do, as a blessing and as beloved. Otherwise he would love us partially, which he cannot. It is a thought, as terrible – and far more – as the last judgement.

The moment we were adequate to any situation, it would be the day of our condemnation (by ourselves), but this also means any day of a sense of guilt, which presupposes that we could and should have been adequate, is the day we retreat from the transcendence.

... The joy of the Orthodox 'fulness of faith' lies wholly in their acceptance of evil into the actual presence of heaven. If you think of the best Anglican tradition, there was far more emphasis on glory then with us, on the continuity of earth to heaven *in as far* as we are likened to Christ – and the *in as far* was the constricting clause which we do not accept, nor which ever enters our head. This measure never occurs, because it bounds about with measures of earthly perception that which cannot be measured by us. We throw it away – the attempt.

March 25th, 1975 [to a friend concerning the ministry of healing]
The exclusion of evil, to me, is always a secondary course, which I am not allowed to seek for myself. We should plunge into it (evil), and work, *from inside*, through it to turn it to good and to joy (so Christ teaches – precisely as he). So suffering and joy will be glory. But this I do not impose nor put up as a universal demand. I but see it as the demand of my life wholly, and of those within its course.

April 13th, 1975
We so easily think that we are 'right', in the heavenly sense, when we are at peace, as if we were babes who are meant to sleep in the arms of God – as if these were our cradle. But never did he promise us that, except in a very hidden core –

which is only the peace of love itself, nowhere else. . . . Why
should we be spared? Perhaps we were spoilt in life by the
tenderness of God to such a degree that we shall be a little
ashamed of how we took it, like children do, for granted.
Why not be a little grown-up now?

May 15th, 1975
You once wrote what heaven means to you and just this
moment I realized that my obstinate refusal of severing the
love of God from human love is precisely, but in a different
image, what you said. How I fought for that – by living. It
makes heaven so desperately small and God finite and eternity pseudo-comprehensible and as you describe divine love
and we swimming in it really means love as the one and only
reality, the air we breathe, the ground we stand upon,
altogether all. But it also means that love is the 'work', being
is the work, and the work is Being. Prayer is not a separate
thing, but just loving to be loved and wanting nothing else.
But love, as being, in itself rules out any separate demands, as
it were love as any extra luxury. That should suit me admirably; I never really wanted anything else ultimately and made
it quite clear.

June 2nd, 1975
This key – what is it? Never less than a simple acceptance of
mental or physical suffering and evil as part of one's life;
unquestioned. To work that through every fibre of one's
existence is a long job.

June 29th, 1975
The other day I watched the seagulls in the sunlight; they
alternate from shining silver to total blackness, when in
themselves they are neither, and thought whether comforting
did not just mean that, to 'see' the others exclusively in their
glory towards which they are created and which they are not
yet except at their entelechies, and to address them as that,
yet in the full recognition of the failure, and quietly carrying
that. It seems the only thing worthwhile on earth, the ever
fresh and ever young joy and travail of transfiguring; and the
final disregard of the surface-unreality now. This is so

difficult where the sociality rules in the Church and we lose the solitude. The true solitude is the true communion, and if one starts an emphasis on the other end one never gets there, because one cannot help making too heavy demands on the others, if the roots in the transcendent life are fading.

July 19th, 1975
The world is burning and has gone beyond the mark where there is time to play about of what is most satisfactory, let alone respectable.

I see the work to be forward so strongly into situations where every scrap of fools' wisdom will be demanded; the only thing that feeds the soul like bread and is never boring and never the same, because it takes up every new situation young and as for the first time. Nothing ever grows old inside the spirit, it aches, groans and weeps, but it is fulfilled and ready for every whisper of the Spirit. I now solemnly know that I have been right when audaciously I demanded that the flesh *can*, in its orbit, truly and enthusiastically follow the spirit, and gladly follow it wherever it will go. And it is my happiness that I can say that with no shadow of doubt or fear. I have run my course in a sort of temerity of love and of faith beyond bounds, following one only vision which wholly absorbed me. There is never any fear in true love. It is not possible. And the truth always wins, even on earth.

July 19th, 1975
I have never bothered about enemies; though I know they exist, and if I took them seriously, would be serious enemies.

September 29th, 1975
I have also been thinking other things, and was flooded with joy, that to the end I am allowed to follow my life's pattern, and need not just only 'go down' and extinguish. I see in that the ineffable tenderness of God. When I was twenty I decided to discover God in my own way, first by disregarding all the Judgement-images, and by only accepting him as love with no limit in every, even the merely earthly, sense and image; and in the faintest reflection of love, I would find him in his 'beggar's cloak' – and the end of the journey brought me to

the beginning of a faith fulfilled in the same blindness. Yet
from vision to vision, and always it was more and more
tenderness of God revealed to me *inside* the human heart; and
expanded more and more within the human limitation. That
is how I chose to love God intensely and with no limit, and
how he allowed me to love him; ever with a divine smile, and
ever as a shared secret; to which (very few) almost none knew
the key. In the wider sense, one could call it a call to the
Communion of Saints; and to what the saints are for us, and
here again we are back in the Canons, where they walk in and
out as persons, fully, and as 'Christs' fully.

And here, inside that tenderness, lies the storehouse of
comfort. It is a jump of blind faith into 'from vision to vision'
inside the blindness. And one must make the blindness one's
joy; and that particular joy one's own secret, which only the
angels know. Whenever I used to cry in desolation, I
thought, Now the angels are smiling again! I let them without a grudge. But the tears had to be wept all the same; only
never the one without the other.

November 3rd, 1975
Yet a fiercer non-answer. Where should we be if we
demanded answers? The only answer can ever be to love and
to love madly, unreasonably, uncounting the cost and looking for no answer − as far as we can, and this is the only
'standard to set' − it can only be set by doing. It is the only
thing that carries one into death, and all else falls away so
lightly as if it had never been.

Christmas 1975
We are wondering why ever more difficulties pursue us to
the limit of endurance, and any new ones brace us up to a
feeling that they come to destroy, and if we do not give them
reality, but march through them, they cannot harm us. It is
not a fairy tale that there are evil forces. Only we refuse to
'attend' to them, but I am crying out for help for us all; or, at
least, for that which is meant to be; and that it should be
achieved. Next year Chapel will live − already for Easter. Till
April it will not be easy, but possible − till we have the whole
house. It will no more be an inhuman situation. It is dark so

soon, and so very dark. Not a sound. I am wondering and wondering. Where are we going?

December 19th, 1976
It does not matter to be hurt. One gets used to that. It is better to remain wide open to every hurt because that is the only possibility of overcoming what evil there is and transforming it.

January 17th, 1977 [to Father Ralph]
We celebrated your novicing day duly with a vigil last night[1] and if the gale had not broken our telephone wire I should ring up, as I want to very much. Then you happily and vigorously took up a medium-sized cross and behold, before twenty years were over, that grew into a monstrous one. That is how heaven showers its graces and compliments and congratulations upon us and all we can do is to wave back and tell them that we well know their tricks and would not really have it otherwise. Well, I'm not so sure if I would not, to wake up every morning in a new fit of terror and worry when I want to enjoy myself. What weather we have had.

June 1st, 1977
You see, with loving one is all the time faced with the demands they are going to make on us in heaven, when really the only reasonable thing is to work towards that. Also, it is exciting, because one more and more learns to hear them smiling in heaven at our clumsy efforts. Of course I don't 'love' everybody, but I know that love is the only thing in the world that makes sense, and I feel a pretty fool where I do not. Nor do I believe in the possibility of disciplining oneself. Love must come from the heart, and it is a matter of stretching one's heart into heavenly measures, but only for love and expectancy of it. We anyway won't be able to escape it!

---

[1] St Antony the Great

VIII THE END-POINT

The death-country – at the gap – Christ

All now resolves into stillness: a sweet and gentle plain: fertile and green: the country of death where the Call of Love is no longer obscured by outside demands. It is the land of intense concentration, leading to the End-point, to the Mystery of Death. The End-point may be seen as the ultimate point of love: the point to which love brings all the suffering, sickness and pain: the End-point is at the gap, beyond which we cannot know. At the End-point, we can only lie before Christ, in repentance. We can only lie prostrate, with our sins, and others', hence the End-point is also the centre, the core of our reality. The gap, the abyss, is no source of fear, for Christ *is* the gap; Christ, incarnate, the Cross, and the Resurrection, does not show the way, nor the door, but he *is* the Way; and he *is* the Door; and his Cross is one from hell to heaven.

[*No date*] *1968* (G)
And now at last the End is almost in sight. My Monastery was not founded as Beginning but as *End*. Wholly under the aspect of the End – the widening out and at the same time the retreating of the End – to the bridge, where the visible changes over into the invisible. And yet just a tiny glimpse is visible.

October 29th, 1968
I find it very absorbing to get old. I mean it gets more and more exciting, heaven coming nearer and a plunge which, the nearer it comes, the less foreseeable it is, the less guess-

able. I think one could train oneself to live for nothing else
but the *faith* in that moment of no-time of nothingness in the
passing through the abyss. More and more I see it coming
like my *one* task in life – to achieve the death, and one can
hardly spare any energy on transient things except what is
demanded clearly.

January 29th, 1969
I felt for one moment in the 'peace of the end' – that at any
moment a beloved voice will say, so homely and so dear: It is
enough now – and lead us into another country, a country
where we are at home, and where all that looks odd and
strange to others now, will fit precisely and prove a glad
preparation and training for it. I think so often of dying, so
immediately and *really*, not as a thing at a distance (though it
might be). I believe training for death means getting up and
rejoicing as at an invitation from God, and how discourteous
it would be to prefer the world or be frightened, or rather, to
mind the silly fears which no one can escape.

August 7th, 1969
A call, a moment's alertness, the bundle packed, and the
journey was done ... what, in advance, one can never feel,
is the help that comes from the other side. Again and again, I
remind myself that death is being done *for* us. We need not
'arrange' it, and yet it is a life's work.... This strange nearness and farness of the other side is so bewildering: the gulf
from our side and the presence from theirs.

June 3rd, 1972 [referring to a young Roman Catholic visitor
and written to the monk who sent him to us]
'Your' pilgrim ... has just left us for his further exploits in
the spiritual universe. He had three days at the Monastery,
obviously happy and, it seemed to me, much in his own
inner Carthusian home. It puzzled him at first, how we unite
without fear, heart and mind, prayer and thinking; how we
integrate the mind into the spiritual life through the *critical*
negation of its inherent claim to autonomy, but not through
exclusion. It is possible in practice, by learning to *rest* in the
'End-point', which is the actual death and the expectation of
it. More and more I find the consciousness of the 'gap'

(which may easily turn into the 'abyss') which we can never bridge in death of ourselves, the source and root of a creative and fearless form of humility; and I am more and more clear in my mind that the going into the desert was not a leaving the world behind, but a leaping forward to learn the convergence in that point without latitude; where yet the whole world *is* in its true being without the fringes. And the Jesus Prayer is for us Orthodox the way towards it and the life inside it.

June 4th, 1972 [to a Roman Catholic monk]
A few days ago, I almost saw the Fathers marching into the desert, and I saw it as a leaping forward – not as leaving a world behind – a world in despair – but forward to learn to live at the End-point where the whole world *is* in its essence, and where the key for its riddles and the solution of its fear lie. That 'gap', which so easily turns into the 'abyss', and the panic of Nothing, is for the monk of the desert his joy. His witness lies *there*; and we owe no apology to the 'world of today', – because we try to live and to learn to live at the very point of its ultimate fear, despair and abyss. It is a point of convergence of *all* – without fringes and frills, and I see the Jesus Prayer as the explicit and purposeful training towards this death-life, in time and no-time; moving more freely, in the Spirit, through the centuries *as* contemporary. Tradition is backwards and forwards – a *personal* meeting, and giving, with persons, on earth and beyond. Have we Orthodox perhaps to offer this? – that we *dare* to let the person develop freely with a little less concern for the ensuing muddles, which again, *sub specie aeternitatis*, are but a sphere for work.

July 1972 [to a Roman Catholic 'active' nun]
Active, so-called, or not, in noise or out of it – so-called – I more and more believe that the daily and homely pain of total failure deep inside is intrinsically linked with the monastic life, and the 'work', if one can call it so, is far less to put the failure right, let alone seek conditions that could eliminate it, than to turn it, the very pain, into joy, somehow, somewhere; anyway, to know that it must be born of free will, or in the fetters of struggling against it.

I had a strong idea the other day. I 'saw' the monks marching into the desert; they said: 'To fight the devil', the power of darkness, which presses in, a spiritual power, a power for which they knew they had no weapons to fight it, for they were still of flesh and could merely endure it. But the enduring meant to stand, or rather, lie prostrate at the point of the End, before Christ, and, as it were, leaping forward to the End, carry the world with them to bring it to that point of Truth, shorn of its fringes, where the world is in Christ, carried by Christ, given meaning by him.

It meant, in a way, to refuse to fight evil on the level of its myriad disguisings, embodiments, mirages, as if it were Person, and to endure it as a spirit-force, in the direct onslaught from outside, but far, far more from inside, from the heart which is inseparably, yet, linked with it.

And then, thinking of the world today, torn apart into two main ideologies: ideologies are spirit, not flesh, in infinite disguises of matters and body, fought on the level of the disguise in the ever-lasting revolution (fascist or communist), i.e. fought in its *ir*reality. And then I see the desert, the Jesus Prayer, as the *being* in that place, deep inside, whatever the noise, where we know that we cannot fight evil, but we can bring it to the End-point and endure it a little more purely there. 'Resist not evil' was a *practical* advice, it can not be resisted, ultimately, to fight is a 'necessary' compromise; but it can be carried.

The Gospel is taking on, with this key, a formidable reality, but it grips one; and, once seen, one cannot let go the vision. Nothing else is interesting any more, when 'it takes over'.

But I want to comfort you. There is no escape, and this *is* the comfort. We are unprofitable servants – and we know it. So let's throw ourselves at Christ's feet and rejoice. It is not 'contemplative' or 'active', only the same reality of pain and failure in a different outward form. It must be carried, and we get stronger by carrying it and heaven becomes more real, the further it seems to go away; and the less we feel it as going. In the last count it only means 'learning to die' in the Gospel sense.

January 22nd, 1973
But, now, heaven happily intervened and released my tormented soul (tormented only in respect to giving talks and travelling about, which came and thrust me into insoluble doubts!). I am hastened into hospital for a cancer operation – the least expected exit! on Sunday; operation next Wednesday in Northampton. This surprise gave me an immense inner uplift, as if a *way* were open again, but for the others it is heavy; our tender and young Monastery.

February 16th, 1973
The whole cancer period (December 31st to February 16th, 1973) was flooded in light and a deep, inward joy of fulfilment and the closing down of many circles and all being precisely right.

February 20th, 1973 (G)
My cancer has solved many insoluble conflicts. Anything less would not have achieved it. Now the Monastery will live. I feel that, even if I die.

August 22nd, 1973
Philosophical consciousness: philosophy prepares for death; acts not on knowledge but on hypothesis which is a partial comprehension of the truth as presented to us in each situation. So there is no final solution, we must always begin again in each new situation. The humble mind is the mind which acknowledges this.[1] Reality is ultimately a *causa* not a *fact*. Thus factual mistakes do not matter so long as the intention is always towards the End-point. At a mistake one does not have to go back, the movement of history is not a straight line but circular (circumstances have already changed when we discover the mistake). To go on in the acknowledgement that all may be continuing senselessness is the final humility which acknowledges the gap beyond which we cannot go, and the going on nevertheless – and constantly preparing for death, so that when the darkness comes we may perhaps just be able to remember a sentence, a word. For in the end not *facts* but attitude (from a *causa*) is what determines.

[1] cf. II, November 12th, 1968 (p. 14)

October 21st, 1973 (G)

Cancer is in the consciousness of life the beginning – the kindly beginning – of death and gives life an intense orientation towards the death that is already there. There is no transitory sickness. For me it has been an infinitely fine thing. Just when I was faced with so many worries, I have from deep within the possibility of not taking them as seriously any more, and often also of finding the funny side in everything.

December 8th, 1973 [to a young Orthodox theological student]

. . . so that at every minute the 'many' might become 'one' at the ultimate point of the world's fear and panic; there alone, it seems to me, can now our work of intercession lie; and be nothing more than what our Matins Canons ever and ever teach us, to lie prostrate before the Judgement of Christ and ask for mercy. Now this has, these last weeks, once more widened – and therefore I delayed so long. I suddenly 'saw' the prophets standing there, seeing the solution 'beyond' – and I saw the true philosophers there – and altogether all the fools – (above all St Paul) of this world. So, where at first stood the desert monks (explicitly), I now see standing the world;[1] and I tried to write it down in a sketch and I now send it to you for Christmas, unpublished as yet. A Cypriot friend asked me for a talk, but 'it should *not* be simple', he said. He was sick of 'simple' sermons, so, you see, I think he got his wish.[2] And, very characteristic of us, I worked a whole week at it, day and night, until it found its shape. The hearers were two young men (merchants), one young wife, a granny who does not understand English, Triphon (two) making his importance known as a rival in shouts of joy and Nicholas (nine) who really wanted to play. Nimmy, the cat, meanwhile brought a mouse into the room where we were, and thus fulfilled the fool's performance! And now I am sweating at another essay on what the Kingdom of Heaven means for us. Perhaps I shall start with the ikons of the Transfiguration and the Descent into Hell. What in *The Fool* I see as the waves of history breaking every minute at the

[1] cf. vii, December 29th, 1974 (p. 92)

[2] *The Fool*: a talk to a small group of Cypriots. Unpublished

brink, where the prophet stands, and so also the waves of dianoetic reasoning, both, in our understanding of the 'Divine Wisdom', as in the 'worldly wisdom' which sees itself as autonomous and fulfilled and one whole, as in all cosmic religions.

The gap is the foolishness of the Cross; without Christ it would be the Nothing, utter darkness. And beyond, wisdom and *dynamis* are one, according to St Paul; what is known by God is loved and is 'life'.[1]

Another way of thinking of it is, two parallel lines in as far as we live in this world. Now, from the one to the other there is a constant commerce – the 'many' into the 'one', and back again, to work in the 'many'. I could see, for instance, the Jesus Prayer like that: the underlying thrusting all into his name, repentant, and, at the very instant, working inside our poor way of finite life: always one after the other, etc. Here I see, perhaps, the most relevant *life* of our Orthodox faith, in as far as world problems are concerned. We *can* never take them seriously, as claims which must *now* be solved; but at the same time, we must work within our limitation of 'many' (and many sins) as best we can. And this 'unprofitable' working is ever the precondition of our deeper abiding inside the eternity life of stillness. This humility of non-demand of that which we cannot do, I austerely demand as a conscious and responsible *attitude* of mind and of heart. I see in humility, and the never-ceasing repentance of what we are perpetrating on the one side of 'world', precisely the *unity* of mind and heart, or the descending of the mind into the heart, as an *attitude*. I intensely reject the idea of *any* esoteric side to the Christian or to the monastic life. What is esoteric (or made so, to sound interesting) must be unChristian and anti-Gospel; and there is never a sign of it in our liturgical texts, which, I think, must be our first guide after the New Testament. They shape us unawares and uncramped, and we must not force ourselves beyond that. The most important things are given us, where we least expect them; and they are, perhaps, if we could see, all the while most abundantly there where we feel ourselves shut out. At the same time the two parallels could also show where the ever-present joy inside the grief lies, which is so much an Orthodox charisma: the

[1] cf. II, October 24th, 1973 (p. 19)

solution is present, and continuous, yet unseen, at moments grasped as solution, then again only believed: *Lord, have mercy*. And, of course, it is all immediately personal. When our Cypriot coachloads from London parishes occasionally come for a Liturgy and lunch (forty to fifty people) on a Saturday or Sunday, I look at the sorrowful old faces, and how far away they are carried in grief-stricken joy of heaven; so near, so far, and then back again into sorrow. This is our Orthodox grief-joy. And we hear every Wednesday and Friday the Mother of God grieve at the Cross. So, again, grief is given a vast spaciousness and may touch joy or may not – but joy is inside the grief, or rather the grief is inside the joy, if it had eyes to see. It is so great a release that our faith nowhere demands the 'exclusion' and shutting-out of sorrow and evil. Ever we are working at it; and so it must be.

December 30th, 1973
A cancer never leaves one. It has entered one's soul and every day is an extra gift. I find it a peaceful condition, because it keeps one's soul on the watchtower, where it anyway wants to be, and so is an immense help for life.

February 16th, 1974 (G)
... all that in the innermost stillness of the cancer experience, which creates a secret apartness even from one's own innermost experiences and at each moment brings one up against the objectivity of death. I find it an infinitely liberating experience – a safeguard against taking things too seriously, good or ill. And also the possibility of opening towards others already becomes easier and more free than before ... so much has happened that I often feel I am watching a film – a flood of people, some of whom I have seen before, others strangers – people of all confessions and also beyond the boundaries of religion, like a breaking through barriers to the central point of meeting where barriers fall away.

March 15th, 1974
But the talk-subject,[1] which almost tore me to pieces in writ-

---

[1] to Anglican priests at Higham Ferrars, later revised and published as *The Realism of the Orthodox Faith*

ing: it was difficult to write, but it ever since is with me like a shining light. I see the End-point – the Transfiguration – inversed in the Descent into Hell all the time; and the contiguity and the forest of crosses, binding hell to heaven and heaven to hell, on every infinitesimal space of earth. It is like an infinite peace of and for the *mind* to think on it, and how, in it, *all* makes sense, *one* sense. As in a work of art, all is without weight in the harmony held. . . .

November 14th, 1974
I often wonder when and how death will come. But everything seems so mathematically 'fitting' that I know it will all be well for us all and precisely right. I only hope the nursing will not be too heavy. I walk again better, but was fiercely exhorted to walk carefully, any bone might fracture. I have not competely found my *work*-balance, except when I am alone, right inside, nowhere else; and there is peace and flooding light.

November 17th, 1974
And now, my whole attention, inwardly, is gravitating towards the Mystery of death. I have another cancer, of spine and left pelvis, and probably more – in most expert hands[1] in Leeds cancer research, where I have to go in ten days for a full examination. I have to 'tread delicately', but I can still walk and am very content to be on the maddest steep slope here, one simply cannot give in to preventives. This – within a year and a half from the operation – means, of course, much. But whatever it means, and will mean (I often think of Barbara),[2] for me it will mean that which is precisely and mathematically 'right', however many groans it will yet demand. In mind and in spirit I am almost over-alert and attentive, and what is not final, retreats. Love grows stronger, wider and wider. Is it a grace, to be allowed to live, or try to live, or make it one's 'work' to live one's philosophy to the ultimate point? I take it as an infinite tenderness of God; although at times I have to take a deep breath not to yield to fearfulness.

[1] Professor Joslin
[2] Barbara Fry

November 20th, 1974
I am continually conscious of a short time left, and so that I don't know which way to turn. I am wanting to turn wholly towards the End, inwardly and totally, still and absorbed in expectation, and then I wonder whether I should use my time rather to the last minute on work done on earth. And between the two, the first is continually winning. Light and darkness are so merged, seeing and not-seeing so closely connected. The only thing I want is to love in wide and great measure, not all the time knocking my head against stupid limitations. And I never in life wanted anything else. I see my way as 'exhausted'.

November 30th, 1974
The cancer ward,[1] where we had to wait, has such a strange atmosphere of peace, like infinite seas of forgiveness. They all will die, they all know they have cancer, and there was that 'mute' suffering. Once in the camp in France I found the same with the Jews who were thrown together inside barbed wire (600) for being shortly deported. There was over them something like a 'total silence' (not one of them could ever be traced) where the End-point stands high and great.

December 1974
To my surprise they were fully up in arms to pray the cancer away. Why? I should not know why. But I leave it to them. I take it as a grace (as I began forty years ago) and as nothing else.

December 19th, 1974
We have to die somehow. There is no other way, and no other freedom we can give to others than by our own death – every day. And not only right but necessary; the world is in agony and it would be too small a task to be dedicated to a successful spiritual campaign. A few *must* go further and accept the End-point as their own ultimate reality. I myself often doubt the appearing serenity of the saints. What did lie behind? What agony of mind and spirit in the appearing deadness of the spirit and the step beyond it? That *one step*. . . .

[1] Cookridge Hospital, Leeds

January 12th, 1975 [from hospital]
One can only prepare in the sense of a centring on the word
'Come', in every relation and tune. Two years ago I experienced the operation as the first definite *invitatio*, to which my
heart could only respond with the hurrying forward and not
a moment's delay or hesitation, or looking backward-
forward; I mean, considering the cost of the running, and
what that stretch might hold. 'I am coming, coming' – to:
'Come up hither.' Now, here, I took my Slavonic prayer-
book which Dima[1] had given me, long used himself and then
put marks into it before I was a nun, for me! There, in the
beginning, he wrote Revelation 3.11: 'I shall come soon' and
'Hold what you have', and the *coming* shifted on to my Lord;
and to the answer: 'Come soon'; and for the stretch it is
enough to 'hold fast' – it is anyway *all* and nothing, but my
constant conscience that I ought to work more, may perhaps
at last rest in the 'holding' which is easy. So, there are four
come(s), and death dissolves into coming; going already as a
negative is overcome, and the circles of 'coming' in death
widen across every painful separation in space, and all goes
out and reverts into ever and ever 'coming soon', also within
our smaller time-eternity steps. And on the very immediate
smaller, or not smaller but just temporal scale, it just says:
Come! But, as you know, I am somewhat practised in waiting!

January 14th, 1975
Today is confirmed that 'the Lord Cancer' has progressed to
the right side of the pelvis – long suspected – it happened in a
respectable amount of pain – and the suggestion of going
over to stronger pain stuff, at least for such emergencies as
whole nights etc! For a moment I panicked because I knew
not where I was, having just readjusted to living (not wholly
willingly, though) and death had moved away. I have now,
with the certainty, regained my serenity and calm, but am
somewhere in the mid-space, so I think. If it were a death-call
it would come with more clarity and force. So, home the bird
flies into my beloved death-country. Today a great peace is
inside me. I see nothing but love.

[1] Father Dimitri

February 14th, 1975
It is one of the days when the time seems suddenly very short and I want to hide my head – die but 'not see' death. There are days when I am totally absorbed in my death-country. One day after Monday, all the measures and values were different from the ordinary course, towards every single being, known and unknown. My heart pleaded for forgiveness; as if a veil were lifted and the mixedness of every breath and thought and action revealed; like a view of the Last Judgement, not terrifying but infinitely releasing; as if now the first step towards glory had been begun. Perhaps one could not live a life with this inside, but I believe the truth is in the uttermost poverty, a hurting and a beatitude-poverty.... I gradually realize where I stand, and just now, of course, I want to see the Monastery, the lovely plans finished and want to run again to the gate and work – and now it comes as a reality that I shall never again be able. And then I turn inward, and there is my wide, immense country, secretly waiting, a place all ready for dying which I love and where I want to be. So one side is end, and the other a young, fresh striding out, discovering what can hardly be expressed; which all comes running to you; looking over to heaven; where I feel a new pull, as if a last impediment had fallen last Monday when I wrote, and the way to *work* is free and fresh and full of curious expectancy.

March 2nd, 1975
Ever from my youth I saw myself working for people in direct contact. I always wanted to be poor and to live with the poor and the first conscious big sense of urgent vocation was that I wanted to 'help people to die'. So many died in my nursing time. I was frightened on lonely night duties. Then I one night decided that I would consider now always death as peace. And I stood by the beds of my patients saying, 'It is peace,' all night. I think, I believe, from then on it was the brink of death both in death and in birth where I alone felt in the right place. The fool was then born. That place seemed the only reality even then, which suited me, when the big things were around, and what was ever infinitely beyond comprehension. Where everything falls away and love with-

out demand counts. . . . I am living in that moment of freedom which I once experienced as 'the peace of the end'. It
was one of my happiest moments, when the past was wholly
gone and the new had not yet begun. And now it is not a
moment but a wide, wide distance of peace and of total stillness which fills me with such happiness that I just cannot
believe it possible. But I believe it could not be possible without the training of darkness; and the endurance of it through
the Jesus Prayer alone; as it were, without content – wholly
bare. Now again, it is bare reality, but so light, full of light
pouring into me, wholly, which wholly absorbs me. I believe
there is a very great deal which must be left behind for
finding the open centre. I mean wrong ideas of what should
be, and should be done. And only that particular darkness can
free us, but it also gives freedom and space to others; that
they can bear the reality from inside, the bare reality.

March 25th, 1975

. . . and the cancer is shedding no shadows – as it has never
for a moment from the start been regarded as an evil, but
only as infinite blessing – and so it still is. There is nothing to
'take away'. Nothing to obstruct a free course, nothing fearful, nothing dark in it.

This is the sum of all my life's work – in mind, spirit, and
in body, and for me, this is a grace; a sanctuary between God
and me; and a place of infinite praise. It, as it stands, can yet
go on for a long time – or not; both will be best.

April 6th, 1975 (G)

How I love the Quintet,[1] the melody which ever wants to go
further and yet is lovingly held and lets itself be held; alone
and not alone, and in the going forward yet at the same time
plays with the others in unity and in full and loving suffering
together, a unity which cannot be fulfilled on earth. It is as if
it were played in the 'centre' – the wide, wide country between earth and heaven – I now live very starkly in this
'between', where, in spite of *many* building worries, the
earthly is already finished and shut away, and the new has not
yet begun.

[1] Franz Schubert, Quintet in C. Major. Cf. June 6th, 1975 (p. xl)

May 6th, 1975

You are a lovely soldier, and – but not before – when you can
see death, not as a potent enemy, but 'trampled down' in
reality – not in dream – and once for all – and the darkness,
the gap of death filled with Christ himself – with the Cross
topfull, where all wounds are healed before they are cut, –
well, ... then you are getting there.... You know, when I
was a nurse, twenty-two, and they died, and I was frightened
on night duty, I, one night, decided to say 'peace' whenever
death was about. So I learned by heart, zealously, in the ugly
face of death to say: 'Death is peace' and I made that my blind
faith (faith otherwise wholly unshaped as yet) and clung to it
all my life as my covenant with God – a sort of private
arrangement – so it is 'forbidden' to talk to me of death as an
enemy, or sickness as anything but blessing. You will just
have to learn that, kick as you may. The conquest of evil, and
of death, is a reality in which we never doubt – a reality that
does cost our life, but is no less reality for that, and can be
turned into good, the moment it is turned towards heaven;
and freely and gladly accepted; instead of manoeuvring it this
way and that to *avoid* it and so lose the vision of heaven that it
would reveal to us, if we would listen; and not act on our
own desires; which ever tend to go at what is only visible and
half real.

May 15th, 1975

It is really quite fun – on the earthly level – to march towards
death. People suddenly take one's eccentricities ever so
kindly! – and to get out of worry (or too much of it) by the
fact that worry might kill one, is also not too bad. Cats
always make a game of everything, turning all things to their
ultimate advantage (so does St Paul in Romans 8, etc.) and
my Mama from childhood called me 'Katzebusi'. And with
Nimmy, it has been proved exact beyond doubt.

August 12th, 1975

I am much lacking in strength and usually lie quietly, centring without words in my death-country and ever inwardly
turning away from the outward things. Images, symbols,
words and expressions go further and further away and what

remains is perhaps simply a total consent to that which I do not know and cannot fathom; except that I feel that sense is all around us and less and less does it matter that we should see it.

October 12th, 1975
It is a beautiful Sunday afternoon – sun and all, and I am 'homesick' and fallen out of the world. You would say 'bereft of words'. And I wonder what the wide land within is in connection to the lostness and lost wondering. Perhaps it is the heavenly Jerusalem seen and believed from out of the 'cruel city' – the earthly Jerusalem. I believe it is with another form of connection (conversation) than words or even feelings. In my death-days, when I lie and have not enough air or something, I seem to lack both, turning away from both words and feelings, and walk in that land very still and in a way free from feeling. So the bereft part of life is not the death-country: and perhaps the dead stillness then makes the inner land wider, stronger and dearer. Only it is difficult to live with it, so growing and growing. For a moment I had a sense that I had come to the end of a heavy and dark passage, more dark even than I knew on the way; and it seems that another part of the journey has begun; less burdened, and more adapted to death positively; homelier with it. What still worries me, and you smile – is that I do nothing (except sewing a bit). I think of reading, and could, and then I turn away before I begin. I want to, and then turn away, as it were; I can no longer afford the time for it.

October 17th, 1975
I am trotting along very quietly and peacefully on my way to the 'heavenly Jerusalem' which for me, as for Plotinus, is very much the joy of total transparence to each other, and never again hedges and frontiers and unsurpassable barriers and infinite spaces to divide and uphold tidy divisions; and various sheepfolds. To break through all that with no longer arousing suspicion! The road is outwardly getting more and more restricted and ever more narrow. I am on five-day courses every five weeks in Leeds Hospital. . . . Next Monday my next ordeal. It means being very ill for two to three

weeks and then much better for two weeks. I can still walk a little, supported, and the pains are not yet excessive – with moderate tablets – but the weariness of body is very hard to bear, and I must keep my heart vigorously still, and am usually just taking my thoughts off, and diving into what I call my 'death-country' – which is the wide open land within, of love with no limits. You comforted me much by saying that, after all, it can also be a release to go outside human words.

February 7th, 1976
One thing always comforts me, the unshaken belief that the last minute is ready, defined and determined unalterably. And *how* the divine determining from eternity is our ultimate freedom, and the ineffable joy receiving us already here into the paradise. Because the last minute hinges this life and the coming together – yet was the Gap; and the fear is wholly joined to the Gap, and the work in life is the work at that, love is that, and hope that. And I believe that as long as the body and mind are vigorous, one should work at nothing else inwardly than facing the Gap and believing beyond it. Then, when weak and impotent, and the Gap yawning, it will yet not frighten, but be recognized as a 'work', gladly done, or rather borne as a task ever undone. I can live for ever in the vision of the three diagrams[1] which so few understand. In life the glad integration of emptiness and blind adherence to reality. But in death it is the same. But far more formidable. And the more one realizes in life the failure, the better one can let go in death, where it is wholly impossible to achieve it. Over that chasm no love and no faith of ours can carry. We must be carried through. Perhaps that is the most important aspect of repentance, the ever-recurring theme song that then we recognize the arms that carried us through, not looking into the abyss.

April 25th, 1976
... and Easter took on a wholly different dimension, of a militant joy inside a fearful tide of sorrow. A joy which is yet

---

[1] *The Realism of the Orthodox Faith*

waiting, inexplorable, sitting concealed inside the suffering and anguish, but *wholly beyond*. Easter – we finished about 12.45, and then had a meal; all whet with death. The resurrection in such an immediate urgency of death and life hides itself inside a determined faith, which will go past every seeming impossibility.

May 16th, 1976
As far as the Monastery is concerned, I have not the slightest doubt ever that my cancer was all for the good of it, although I should love to work a lot. I cannot even walk to the farthest field.

October 17th, 1976 (G) [to Doris Keller, who sent a gift of records]
I always enjoy your records again. I like the Third Suite[1] best. The transcendence of the melodies of the trumpets, the wonderful harmony in between the joy of the dances and of the eternity. I want 'harmony', and strongly disciplined – it is something releasing for the poor body which has been transformed into a double battlefield, here the cancer and there the anti-cancer pills. The last one is worse. The cancer at least belongs to oneself.

January 8th, 1977
I love the Epiphany texts. They are most akin to Holy Week. I always see the Jordan stretching down into the abyss of death when Christ entered it, down and ever further down into the tomb where I first found Christ living, and I in his immediate presence. I know it happened and is still real and often I stretch forward to that clear sight, when now the shadows near me lengthen. What will it be when the veil is forcefully torn away and the Truth alone to rule? But I have also a strong feeling that wading through darkness now belongs irrevocably to the journey and that I must take this often in this void without alarm. Christ did not die comfortably, and at the moment I feel gently led into the pre-death battle, so I cannot expect an easy journey.

[1] J. S. Bach, Suite No. 3 in D Major

April 1st, 1977

I am reading a book on Russian mystics and writing a review[1] and I feel in a sense miles away; as if it were a life which I had passed through and do now no longer believe in. But it has formed me. I am altogether indifferent to any 'spiritual writing', it seems bare; so let's go up to Jerusalem and up and up and up and up.

June 1st, 1977

What an exciting journey you have in front of you. We have pictures of St Catherine's Monastery – Sr Katherine always thinks of it as her own! – and the arduous ascent to the Moses Mountain. Someone, a monk, brought us a crystal from there. It is good that you will have an experienced guide and it will all pour in through your skin – all the many centuries of spiritual peace and spiritual warfare and the very earliest monks, and the very tenderest beginning of the Jesus Prayer tradition will there come to meet you, if you can forget the noise and – for the monks – the torments of the tourists. And the Bush, may it burn for you, and fill your heart with joy and gladness. I shall be thinking of you there. I am always so compassionate for the monks, who in the uttermost desert of deserts – have less peace for prayer than we here, only a mile away from the milling crowds of Robin Hood's Bay. You will feel in the Monastery how time is within eternity, and everything that is relevant in the realm of the spirit is ever present and can never be lost, we have but to open our heart, and it comes to meet us.... How little we know of the significance of things and ever more strongly comes the knowledge that the meaning lies on the other shore and from there we are tenderly guided – and what seems now incomprehensible may at a moment be turned into meaning and joy. On Mt Sinai it all goes up and up, as if the world were already left behind, and one stood at the very brink of eternity, on a slender bridge, calling upwards, where we cannot yet reach except with the eyes of the soul – and in faith. And how austere is the Spirit where it meets us directly and bare, and so deeply nourishing.

[1] *Russian Mystics* by Sergius Bolshakoff: in *The Mouth*, August 1977

IX THE MYSTERY OF DEATH

And so, face to face with death, we return to the consent of
the mind, the joyful acknowledgement of the limitation of
thinking. We do not *know* what lies beyond life. But, in the
not-knowing, we gladly believe that it will not be the sad
repetition, nor modification, of all that we know.

Holy Week, 1953
Infinite hope for hell in that stillness of death. There are no
enemies. He said it himself.

September 13th, 1955 (G) [to a friend of her youth]
Later in the evening a thought came to me which astounded
me. We two wept all our tears that we were not loved
enough and adequately, and these were 'right' and 'legiti-
mate' tears. But after a few years in heaven everything will be
turned round; and we must put all into the utmost effort to
widen so that we can bear the overmeasure of being loved,
and that the joy of it does not kill us. Imagine the *Communio
Sanctorum*, what a strength of loving will suddenly come
down on us. That is the 'other side'; when it gains reality,
then we shall sing quite other melodies.

August 1965
The only thing we know by experience is that sometimes
there flow from things, which in themselves are incom-
prehensibly hard, streams of light and blessing. We have to
bend under the not-knowing because we do not know what
immensities open up after death. What we are preparing for is
bigger and of a different order, of wholly different standards

118

and values from that which we know now. We do not even know what love is when it is able to manifest itself *wholly* in another, apart from what it is here on earth, where it can in its fullness only become real in and by the overcoming of evil.

May 1st, 1967 [to explain why we pray for the *rest* (repose) of souls]
That which is right at the other end – the consummation – is to grow into the likeness of Christ; so that his divine life *is* our life, but what that means we do not know; one thing we do know is that it is divine, and therefore there can be no passivity in it; no passive resting, but an overwhelming activity and *creative* power of love, which we shall *be* – not have.

Now, coming from the world, the first thing a human heart will have to learn is to be quiet and very still and to cease from piecemeal activity, cease from aims which are limited and passing, cease from everything which is not pure love, being stripped of all the trappings which are not totally true. This is the precondition for the creative love, and is in itself the highest form of creative activity which *we* can conceive, i.e. the non-activity in our human and thwarted sense. That means, for this we *can* pray. We can somewhat conceive it, but for what comes next we cannot pray. 'Peace' is the highest word we know for that condition, where we *are* what we *do*, and *are* what we *love*, and *are* what we *know*. Where to know and to be known is only one thing, indistinguishable, to love and to be loved equally one thing – the total simplicity in total stillness which at the same time is total absorption and *work* inside Love.

That means 'rest and peace' are only human, inadequate terms for becoming *love* in one's total essence.[1] But this, in a way, is also total sacrifice where it is lived and acts on earth, within finite measures. The earth cannot hold the divine way of life without inflicting on those, who want to live it, deadly wounds. It cannot be helped; but these wounds *can* be suffered and turned towards that life which they signify and where they are pointing to. If we were just happy and

---

[1] cf. v, April 3rd, 1968 (p. 62) and April 11th, 1968 (p. 62)

humanly fulfilled on earth all the time, we should have a
desperately long way to go on the other side; first of all to
wake up to another form of happiness, less direct and more
costly, and secondly to accept the way to it; which does hurt;
and does cost one's life.

I mean something *very* clear, but to express it is not so
easy. But we shall see you soon.

May 11th, 1967
... the ceasing of our finite ways of activity when we *are*
what we do, know and love. 'Rest' and 'peace' are only
inadequate expressions for the divine activity.

June 20th, 1967 [a conversation on death, with a bricklayer]
... Then B: 'But we cannot be certain – not quite certain';
then I answered, would it not be terribly sad if we *knew*? for
that would mean that it would again be something as small as
our minds and this life.[1] And B. took it and said, it was true,
and there was a peace when people died, which was nowhere
else. The peace which passed understanding. And I said that
at last we would reach our final beginning – not always begin
and begin again, but BEGIN. I was amazed, and I shall never
forget this ... which gave me a sudden realization that
Christian Platonism is that which minds, who think and who
can no longer take the everlasting assertions of the Church,
need and love and which has a force of consolation which no
assertion can ever convey. But can one put it forward? Is it
teachable, other than as an answer to an endeavour; to an
anguish and need?

May 24th, 1968
If only I had the steam I had ten to twelve years ago for
writing. But my strength must be going somewhere. It is so
flowing out of me that there seems not enough reservoir for
writing. It needs heaped-up strength for writing.... How
often I used to think – now I still would have the strength to
write, will it be for long? And now every scrap I did produce
is so necessary and I cannot enlarge it. I am now in a different

---

[1] cf. II, June 29th, 1967 (p. 12)

world, a world, in a way, of steeper austerity where writing is not possible. Then I rested inwardly in the vision, and now it needs every scrap I have to work it out in my life. It is a consolation that this life is only the preface to the real life and that the beginning, chapter 1, is on the other side, and who knows, there may be very many chapters following there.

January 29th, 1969
Now it is evening and the day is over. It was a quite beautiful grand sunset, transfiguring us with a promise of a world beyond, and glories beyond, and REST beyond; I don't mean just 'rest' but Rest that *is* Work, and Work that *is* Rest, because it is the same as we are.

September 11th, 1969
I think constantly of dying; and often relive that moment of hearing the call: prick up the ears, and run, run, run towards it with wide open arms to the new, the wider, the fuller life; though the step into it never loses its terror, as if it *could* not be taken. But death is dead, so it *must* be possible to take it, and each time it somehow seems almost 'natural' when someone dies. It is a transformation we so deeply long for, and yet know it not at all.

June 16th, 1970
There are so many already on the other side; it becomes more and more exciting looking across the ridge – we just get far enough to peep with one eye over it into vast distances of a landscape so full of peace, work and glory.

[No date] 1972
Don't grieve. In heaven we shall get the most incredible surprises. Oh, they have such a sense of humour in heaven; *that we know*, and as we let them play it freely, it is surprising what comes out.... It is amazing what death does to one and how the most unlikely people are near and shine in glory. How little our fringes and moods matter for heaven.

February 11th, 1975
I believe we are at a new starting-point; I cannot think what it will be in heaven when these new starts will be new and

quiet, and not year-long agonies of inch-by-inch turning. I am looking forward to something ineffably young, only when I was young I was never as happy as now.

February 16th, 1975
We can see so little of the ultimate Truth of our life; if we did, perhaps we could not endure it. One day, we shall, and then the help of the new life is part of us – the Presence of Christ, our Judge and our Saviour, will enable us to endure the moment of recognition of all our failure and sin, which I feel more and more acutely, but in infinite peace.

May 25th, 1975
And I thought the other day, all our earthly life, in the eternity light, may appear to us like a nursery, and all the great tragedies and pains we felt, just like the very small beginning of that which is infinitely greater and perhaps also far, far more demanding. In a way I am looking forward to that, but the passage still seems like a difficult journey; as in the mountains, one gets up at night, and the mountains look terribly austere, like ghosts, and one is frightened but also thrilled. I am often wholly absorbed in the expectation of death, and I feel all the preparation from childhood has not been too much, and I am glad for it, the actual outcome is *so* insignificant, only the working, the effort and the love for the work counts, nothing else. What people think is so infinitely ephemeral, today this, tomorrow the opposite; and useless to all of us anyway. I thought on Friday, how my vision of life had always been to comfort, and I felt a store of comfort in my heart, which somehow never came to the full working. So I am expecting the work of comforting to begin in proper measure the other side – and this would feel fitting to the preparation of the life-pattern here on earth. It is all so absorbing, and a mass of things unknown, waiting directly before my nose, and I cannot 'see', only 'feel' it present. One can only throw oneself wholesale into the arms of God, and that is not a mean place to be, but a place of infinite 'rest' – where rest and work will be the same, because in heaven work will be just *being*, and not endless conscious effort and more and more effort.

September 17th, 1975
I have just heard that my sister Marthy died this morning in her sleep. Alice happened to be there – in the nursing home – watching ... the release tender and gracious. How the solutions come sweetly from heaven.... In my last birthday letter to her, something made me write the first lines of a Methodist hymn of my youth, which is often with me:

> Look, from the West light is shining,
> And in the evening, brightness....

This morning, feeling nothing of it, I sat very peacefully reading my beloved 2 Corinthians 3–5, and all of glory and weight of glory, and faith as spirit – and glory-spirit, faith, death and life. And it is so strange how death lifts us up into a world of freshness and space and lightness – although one can't help weeping for the joy and movement of it. A little push and one is in a different dimension, so unknown and yet so intimately known and infinitely loved and ever and ever believed; for which one would give the whole of oneself.

January 5th, 1976
I am ever preoccupied in my mind with something I do not see. I can hardly take off my attention, when I am alone. Perhaps it is my End-point without latitude. It feels like doing nothing, and incapable of doing anything, and is quite difficult. *All* the values have vanished into non-judging, stretching forward to new measure and vision. I ever think that if all the worlds showed me that heaven was not, I would still blindly believe out of love; against any reason, but never against Reason, which for me *is* love. I had a book on death sent to me, full of existentialist reasoning. I detest the approach of illuminating the Mystery by human reasoning.

February 5th, 1976
It is always a deeply comforting thought that the ultimate minute on earth can never be an arbitrary minute, but will fit precisely that pattern of life which we can as yet not see, but which is wholly our very own and at the same time infinitely greater than we are – where we are sheltered in the very big pattern of all, living inside the divine world – and 'face to face'. What will this 'face to face' mean! and what surprises

are waiting for us. It is a grey, cold, misty day. I just thought, what will it mean when a shaft of light will hit us from another world, and gates are opening, one after another, into further and ever further distances; now so unknown to us – we hardly reach the hem of his garment; and yet are already inside him.

March 21st, 1976
And looking at the lights of Whitby the other day, I was thinking how lovely it would be, if it were the heavenly city, so near, and already in sight; and no more world; and wider faculties of seeing and understanding, with less troubles ever to mar the vision and the joy.

April 25th, 1976
I am much preoccupied by the sense of a colossal attack, worldwide, on the innermost kernel of the Christian faith. And therefore many frills have to go. I see the attack closing in very fast, and this may well be at the root of these unbearable attacks of fear: what will become of us?

I must tell you more about it when you come. It is strange that today it has so come up to the surface. The readiness of personal sacrifice on the totally militant, anti-Christian front is so great, that I always think that in eternity it might in a moment topple over into its contrary, and 'the last shall be first'. I often wonder in what scene our life is involved without our knowing it. Certainly much remains hidden from us, and we are entrusted with a few inches of earth to play our part. It is – in the programme – a definite and clear universal attack on love. And, therefore, the 'key' of the Gospel is now so urgently needed. To regain that field of reality, where evil is not met on its own level of fighting, and shifting unreality.

December 3rd, 1976
Heaven seems so near in the stillness of snow; and I begin, in a way, hardly to differentiate any more between letters and visits – they seem equally close and it will be nice to have better capacities on the other side and to pour love into the world, if God will give it to us to do. It is never in our own hands or choice, but that is a lot safer than if it were. I often

wonder what it will be when God will take away all our narrow earthly bonds and we readjust to a life wide and free; when, fully and totally, our being will be our work. It will be nice when a bell rings over the pastures and all the fields will look upwards.

December 19th, 1976
Let us think of heaven and how in a moment everything will be wholly changed. Reproaches will not reach us and we shall be able to stride out wherever the soul is capable of going and all that befalls here will have meaning of peace, not of war and instead of walking inside one's own orbit of thought we walk inside thoughts that are higher than ours.

March 4th, 1977
It is night and very still. I am all inwardly wondering and amazed at the way others meet death so 'confidently'. To me it comes as labour, but with no hesitation, no, not a motion of it in my heart. So many untellable things I want to say. Perhaps from heaven I shall be able to.

June 1st, 1977
Perhaps to die is not so big a step ... every day we get nearer the end of life's journey and towards our new 'youth'.... I always think that we shall be young, but without the calamities of youth.

June 25th, 1977 (G)
So all my vital strength comes to my help at the end and death is so completely integrated that it is rather a little bridge to my new youth. I always think that we shall be eternally young, but in maturity – free from all the pains and labour of growth.

X HER WRITING

Words and imagery are the most delicate vehicle for the transference of thought. Writing is an art of creation and holds within itself something of the Mystery of the Spirit, a part not open to analysis and with an autonomous influence of its own, as it were beyond the author's intention. Once committed to words, the author's thoughts seem to work on their own. A book, however, should never be the instrument of *direct* teaching: it may only hint in image. All is as poetry, the breath of a clue, a spark to extinguish in mid-flight or to blaze into fire.

When we knew that Mother Maria might die, one day I was afraid. Suppose I should *forget*. 'But,' she said, 'how can you? It is all in my books.'

Published Works
Platonism and Cartesianism in the Philosophy of Ralph Cudworth
The Hidden Treasure
Sceptrum Regale
Evil in the New Testament
The Jesus Prayer
Ralph Cudworth: Mystical Thinker
Amos, Prophet of God
Orthodox Potential
The Psalms
The Realism of the Orthodox Faith
An Introduction to the Divine Liturgy
'Ralph Cudworth' (an article in *The Month*, June 1976)

Unpublished (major material)
'Poems and stories of Jeremiah' (translation)

126

'Poems of Isaiah' (translation)
'The Book of Genesis' (chapters i-xv, exegesis)
Notes on the Cambridge Platonists (Cudworth, Smith, Whichcote)
Notes on Hooker
Notes on Anglican Divines
Philosophical Essays
'The Fool' (a talk)
Translations from Gauss's *Handkommentar zu den Dialogen Platos*
'Plato and the Orthodox Church' (uncorrected)

December 17th, 1959 (G)
The book[1] has sixty pages; Fr Lev, who studied it sentence by sentence, found I could just as well have written thirty or forty chapters instead of three, and with that have made the reading easier. But I believe three chapters are quite enough, because the story must affect everyone on his own – in the form which is personally adequate and intelligible. Therefore, hints, when they are clear, are sufficient. So I lived totally in the Gospel during several weeks when I was writing; I could see all and touch it from inside; and in spite of being from time to time in a real creative anguish, it was nevertheless a very happy and full time. I often wonder why one cannot simply transfer this to other people; but that it is not possible, we may see only later and understand. Often I long very strongly that the Gospel might be wholly real and 'contemporary', and present, so that you could walk, dance and sing in it as your very own, your One and highest. But it may be that I am impatient for that.

[No date] 1960
I have written a 'book' last summer and one this summer[2] and I think with that my life's work is achieved! Both books are on love and the overcoming of evil by love. The second is on love in married life and on love in monastic life.... If one is not oneself caught up in the thousand entanglements of

[1] *The Hidden Treasure*
[2] *The Hidden Treasure* and *Sceptrum Regale*

outward family care, one has it perhaps easier to see the dry bones and how it all makes sense in the eyes of God and is a work, in which *he* himself acts, is present and rejoicing over every scrap of true sacrifice. And how the things which may often seem small and without meaning, gain magnitude and presence in their relationship to our everyday cares. So I have tried to comfort those who are married simply by showing them God in their life, a married life – and God's joy over it all; and that therefore no special reward is needed, or special 'treat' to find the true fulfilment: for the fulfilment is love, and love can be most truly lived in sacrifice, be it now in a happy or unhappy married union. The scope for sacrifice remains wide for all, and is wider still in a seemingly unfulfilled life, when every single day is a task to be taken up; and laboriously to be done and suffered. And the goal is not anything to be attained in this life, but in heaven. Our journey is but a training for the bigger things and the one thing, and the one only thing which matters is never to cease to love, one way or another, since it is love and our readiness to love which opens heaven for us and prepares us for our final end: to take our place in the Communion of Saints, there to live love fully and without any reserves or concerns for oneself.

October 24th, 1960 (G)
The book[1] is not a treatise, as it seems, but a poem and must be read as a whole. For myself it has the significance of total reconciliation with all and with everyone that I have met in my life.

October 30th, 1960 [to Professor Baumgartner]
I have now almost finished the Isaiah text – i.e. those passages which you had chosen in the Isaiah lectures; and the prophet rises from out his poems in a strange power and almost terrifying. The colours have come out strangely dark, sharp and terrible; and I believe it needs an accompanying text, to make it possible that the great comfort may be found, which you saw in such a wonderful way. These two little volumes of

[1] *Sceptrum Regale*

Jeremiah and Isaiah poems are so akin and yet so totally
different. The personal nearness of the prophet Jeremiah, that
part which one can experience with him and do with him, is
lacking in Isaiah and this fills one with a sense of awe and
anguish. With Isaiah one may only pour oneself out into the
greatness of his vision; and in this losing oneself – without
any claim of comfort – to find *the* comfort which is beyond
feeling and even understanding. I often wonder where I have
the connection between the OT and the NT. I find something in myself, which you woke up, and which I do not find
anywhere else. It is the very personal relationship to the
prophets; something familiar in them, which I love with my
whole soul; or rather, I believe, I love themselves uncondi-
tionally and totally. I ask them to let me in, and I feel they
like this prayer; and carefully, step by step, they fulfil it. But
the relation to the NT, I believe, I don't have it as much in the
text itself, as in the prophets as persons; as they live now, and
as that which they are now; guiding us. I see how they found
in Christ their maturity rejoicing; the beloved Mystery which
they had ever sought and which in pieces, in many particular
contradictory pieces, they had to live. I see how Christ put
his own life, which transcended all human measure, into the
succession with the prophets and thereby he integrated them
into his own life. It was a deed of infinite love and self-
emptying, which we can contemplate only by worshipping
it. He put himself into the ranks of the servants of God, who
already understood themselves as friends and beloved. So I
see the relation between OT and NT as a deed; in time, but
with eternal meaning. Something exultant, dynamic and
spacious, and at the same time very still. Something which
gives widest scope to research, scope so wide and so deep as
is the love of God itself. In this relation of OT and NT I see
something greater than that which our fathers[1] had, when
they were thinking in one straight line, and the "Word of
God" was to them a book of literal authority; and an external
truth. So it seems to me that with the research we have not
lost anything but have indeed gained *all*. . . . The second subject is the overcoming of evil. After my first devil I felt more

[1] Protestant biblical scholars

and more that I had found the key to the understanding of the
Bible. And when our Abbess asked me to write on 'How to
read the Bible', I thought I could do nothing better than to
give them this key to the centre; the task of love in the
world.[1] In the third chapter I describe how this task was lived
by Christ, St Paul, St Peter and St John, and the Mother of
God. The third chapter is full of an inner serenity and *Lieb-
lichkeit*. A St Paul as the Protestants don't know him, and as
only one can guess him who loves the OT. The Eastern
Church has an entirely different St Paul from the West.

It has come out a strange book, with a strong dynamic
force in all the spheres at once. The unity of mind and heart I
have never been able to show as I have here. I consider this
book as my life's work, although it has only seventy small
English pages typed in wide spacing. . . .

[*No date*] *1961* (G)
Never, as here, has it become so clear to my consciousness
that the *Sceptrum Regale* is a poem. . . . I have not the least
intention to teach. I don't want a psychological discussion, or
clarification, or to be a guide. *Sceptrum Regale is* in a simple
sense, as life *is* in its most true being. There is no reason at all
to discuss it. It always seems to me that it is a fact which one
can accept or not. But there is no question of agreeing about
it or not. That at least is how I feel. Somewhere it must be
very deeply connected with my innermost being; because
everything to do with it goes to my heart. Here I have gone
to the uttermost limit, because I was seized with a strange
'total compassion', I wanted to give people something big of
warmth, of fervent hope, and a love which can be wholly
trusted. I wanted to lift off from them for a moment the
burden, so that they could breathe again in astonishment at
the 'new', as if it were just there, and had even begun for
them. And because it *has* just begun, it is not a lost paradise
which I described, it is a 'present' paradise which carries and
refreshes each one, whether we want to see it or not. The
keynote is that I wanted to comfort, to comfort *at any cost*.
And then the work is carried by quite another intention, or

[1] *The Hidden Treasure*

rather, a more particular one inside the whole. I suddenly 'saw' that the two basic forms of the life of a woman mutually open themselves one to the other, move towards each other, and that from such an opening an unexpected help could arise, a deeper understanding and a quite new joy of one's own way, if it is so seen within the whole, and that the fulfilment rests in the whole, and becomes realized in each outward situation, and that happiness no longer depends upon outward circumstances. 'Fulfilment' is something much greater, and for everybody the 'table is prepared'. In order to discover this kind of 'opening' I went down into the innermost bare significance of marriage, and also into the bare content of monastic vocation. It is for me ever and again a strange surprise how the tears in *Sceptrum Regale* are not seen at all by people, or felt by them. They see only the joy and feel something un-understood which goes to their hearts. When I described marriage, I was suddenly frightened: did I not choose colours which are too dark? would people be frightened? And you read it as a winged paradise. But this is how it is, and the pains appear only as joy and love; that is for me the greatest fulfilment and comfort. The paradise is a total sacrifice.

[*No date*] *1962* (G)
Yet the writing times are the happiest and for two years I have longed secretly for it again, and am forever seeking for a push, or someone who will simply force me to write. But perhaps for you writing is not quite such a frantic effort, and comes more naturally and easily than it does to me, where everything has to climb up through so many layers until at last it reaches the head and can be set in order.... How helpless one is when one attempts to communicate the simplest inner experience. And then, would it help anyone? If it doesn't shine out directly through one's whole being, and also anything at all one writes, would words be effective? I think over that a lot, and come again and again up against a barrier. Cudworth himself once said that the spirit didn't allow itself to be 'smeared' with ink on paper, but expressed itself best in action. And he regarded words as mere 'signs'; the spirit depends upon the other's spirit reading him, by

means of the words, across the words. I believe that is possible to a quite remarkable degree with Cudworth. There is something hidden in his words which takes hold of one again and again with the utmost force and gives the feeling that beyond the words lies a fairyland if only one could find the 'Sesame, open thy door'. (Fairyland, of course, means for me the real world, the wholly real Kingdom of Heaven, and not a figment of the imagination.)

September 12th, 1964 [to Professor Armstrong]
May I present you with my only printed[1] essay. I have recently written a short complementary essay on 'The Mystery of Christ in the Philosophy of R. Cudworth';[2] based chiefly on his magnificent sermon of 1647. I wrote it at the request of Hasso Jaeger, a Catholic scholar and friend of Père Bouyer. There I tried to show the link between Platonism (based on the later works of Plato after *Parmenides*) and the contemplative life. In writing I became more fully conscious of the consequences in Cudworth that he had not taken enough account of the dialectic in Plato. But the essay is still in German. I should be intensely interested in what you think and if you do not read German I will translate it.

You will see that my interpretation of Cudworth rests upon a definite interpretation of Plato. I have had the immense privilege of studying several years under Prof. Hermann Gauss, now in Bern; he has just accomplished the six volumes of a commentary on the *Dialogues* of Plato [*Handkommentar zu den Dialogen Platos*. Bern, Herbert Lang]. A true Platonist, he is of course also extremely isolated; and since he does little himself to get known, he is of few understood. This is my foundation, and never since have I found anything which could shake it; although since fourteen years I grew entirely independently from him.... And now since a year, by the encouragement of H. Jaeger, I am trying with all my might to work myself into more intensely philosophical tasks again. I should like to discover in a very careful study the Platonism (perhaps rather as attitude of life) which

[1] i.e. *typed*
[2] translated, revised and published in 1973 as *Ralph Cudworth: Mystical Thinker*

underlies the theology of Hooker; and if this were possible, to gain some clarity on his position between Thomas More and Erasmus on the one hand and the Cambridge Platonists on the other. I do not agree with Munz on this question; and Catholics now seem to claim him as an exclusive Aris- totelian. I am not far advanced yet with it. I so easily sink back into the feeling of having nothing to say; which would fit anywhere; and that perhaps there is no need of writing as long as thoughts are lived; and also suffered. But in this I am not sure of the part which sheer 'laziness' plays. Writing is a desperate effort to me!

September 1965
The question of the symbolism of language is one which interests me deeply as a Platonist (and it has a large part in my presentation of the Cambridge Platonists). I love Cudworth's idea that words are vehicles, but which incite the spirit to a self-active reproduction of truth by participation in God. The transference from one soul to another is a sovereign com- munion of the spirit, a mystery which is not dependent wholly on the words, which are always inadequate and must be so. On the other hand, in meditating upon it, I am always deeply moved at the tender condescension of God in entrust- ing himself to human words, in limiting himself to such a degree that we may 'touch' him.

October 4th, 1965
The Hidden Treasure does hold my life – *is* me – my work and all – *in nuce* – that I can offer. When this is 'known', I am safe.

February 1966 [to Sister Thekla]
It makes me happy that you love my Psalter[1] – it is *so* much part of my own life and soul; so much *me*. 74, 71, 77, 90, 139 and 88 (the dearest of all).

February 6th, 1966
It is the surface – to stitch through the surface. That is why it will be so important to write *for you*. It is almost untold

[1] typescript copy. We still use it in Chapel

torment to me to write for 'people' – but for you there is no
surface, and that is why it will flow again; when I need not
adapt to an alien reader – or rather, see his dull and staggered
and blank face at reading me!

August 1st, 1967
Last night, walking into the hut ... it suddenly hit me that I
would never, never, feel safe again in life; I mean safe as I was
in the Abbey, in my cell, and not even the cell exists any
more, not only my safety – and then I wondered how I could
ever write any more.

November 12th, 1968
For the phenomenal world one has to stick to the 'becoming',
the instability of the movement that renders it partly
unthinkable. The moment of discovery that we have no
direct access to the things, and the accepting it, is a very
freeing thing. Only through thought can we grasp it. Cudworth's Plastic Nature really only defers the problem on to a
lowest intellectual power, but the bridge is not built. As a
working principle Plastic Nature certainly is excellent. It
always works, and the things richly reward the
respect.... At the end of the fourth chapter[1] you will have
to insert the 'Mystery'.[2] What I then did not completely see,
sitting too absorbed in Cudworth's mind, was what it means
to assume the eternity of the ideas *as we think them*; that is, the
lack of dialectic thinking, whenever we apply the ideas to the
explanation of our affairs; – and how in the end the eternal
damnation came out.

   Of course, I am a bit sorry I did not see it then straight off.
It would have made a lovely chapter.

January 29th, 1969
I wonder whether just one tiny bit the wind might change
when the book is out. Now, my life and I are always considered apart from my life's work, as if writing were a child's
play, a luxury, a pastime, and cost nothing. Then of course it
looks odd, etc. – and sometimes I sit down and would weep

---

[1] *Platonism and Cartesianism in the Philosophy of Ralph Cudworth*
[2] *Ralph Cudworth: Mystical Thinker*

over it. But when 'the peace of the end' came into sight for a moment, then I knew again that in the end it *will* count, it will weigh like a full day's work, and will not be passed over so lightly. My whole life I have again and again poured into my writings, to give the very best I was, and all, all I had – and then it still looked selfish. *How* easily the spiritual work is discarded as not-work.

October 9th, 1969
I suddenly saw the way of work: the overall theme is, in what way the Orthodox and Platonic *attitudes* coincide. But our way is not in studying the tradition in endless scholarly comparisons, but from the Plato-Gauss, i.e. from Plato himself (with Gauss's 'geography') to draw and find new lines, new aspects *straight* out of the Gospel. In short, what Gauss himself meant to write next.... This will be 'out' and 'away' enough from ordinary writing to rouse my spirits to set out, here again in the total non-direction towards any public, which alone is my precondition of work.

October 29th, 1969
The things which live on are almost always those which are not immediately recognized. The non-recognition is a safeguard. If they are recognized, then they stop as if they could not grow any more. If a book is taken up for a few years it means that it is written to those few years, which pass so quickly. I have always an idea, quite definite, but hardly expressible, that the breaking away from what they think is tradition and the *HT*[1] somewhere far away will meet. I mean, when a return to transcendent values occurs, the *HT* will be a language they will be able to accept. It is that hidden Platonic *core* of the unity of mind and heart inside the tradition which can never be killed, because the form of *expression* will always be adaptable, without the core and substance being lost.

December 5th, 1969
I *know* it more and more that I am writing forward, skipping perhaps a generation; but even that is doubtful.

---

[1] *The Hidden Treasure*

December 17th, 1969
And the symbolism of language: reflection, *sign*, but never adequate, for if it were, the eternal would be imprisoned in the finite and the finite crushed and stagnated by the Absolute.

[No date] 1972
I do hope that if you review it, you will bear in mind that *The Hidden Treasure*, as well as all the other books, is the explicit outcome of many years of monastic seclusion and may, therefore, not conform easily with what might be regarded as 'normal' in formal academic, philosophical, or theological writings. You will see for yourself how concise all our writings are and how carefully they avoid direct teaching.

July 10th, 1972 [to a bookseller friend]
I fully appreciate the demand for patristic textual criticism, particularly in Oxford, but, as I indicated in our introductory circular letter, this is not our primary purpose.

We take our first commitment to be that of publishing books of living Orthodox *thinking*, that is, not the interpretation of *thought*. This means that the thought of the Fathers and the tradition of the teaching of the Church is, as it were, taken for granted, having been totally assimilated and integrated into the substance of the *thinking*. Thus, we believe that it becomes possible, without repetitive expansion and explanation, for the books to speak actively with the voice of Orthodoxy on common contemporary problems, as it were both inside and outside the problems of the West, inside as sharing them, and outside as speaking out of the tradition and attitude of the East.

This does not necessarily preclude some overt academic studies later, if we can afford it, but I must insist that our first call is this sending out of books *as* Orthodox and not merely about Orthodoxy. Secondary writing cannot for ever satisfy thinking and interested minds and, in the last count, if such secondary writing is the only meeting-point for the West and East, Orthodoxy will become relegated even to a sterile condition as only to be seen in relation to the West for vis-à-vis comparison or information.

Orthodoxy is the living bread for thousands and it has something to offer to the West in its particular attitude of heart and mind. It is not a theory or a museum-piece! Our one claim is that our books reflect a faith which is *lived* and thought out into actual life; they reflect the unity of religion and everyday experience which is so true to Orthodoxy and not as well-known in the West. If our readers catch something of this, then they will know more about Orthodoxy than they could otherwise; the so-called strangeness and not fitting any compartment is already a lesson in itself!

Of course we do not expect to make money or be popular, but, if only one or two benefit, that is all we hope.

Thank you for your concern and help. I am grateful.

September 25th, 1973
The Hidden Treasure has a history. In 1947, in my university years (I studied after eleven years' nursing first) I wrote *Evil in the New Testament*, informally called 'the Devil'. This was a careful text research, which during the Holy Week and Easter, when I wrote it, burst down upon me like a blinding vision. I thought I would have to burst under it, of joy, that 'the Gospel made sense', active sense, and that 'salvation' is a call and open door to a *creative* attitude for *all* – in the working with evil.

Then for twelve years I laboured, and tried to rewrite it in a less academic form, and at long last *The Hidden Treasure* emerged and leads further, and *Sceptrum Regale* is a continuation of it, an application, as it were, in one sphere of many.

The last two essays in *Orthodox Potential* are the uttermost point of continuation of the 'vision' of 1947. *Eastern Spirituality* I wrote in 1970, and then explicitly saw the diagram, and since then the End-point rules all my thought, as it had before, but now more clearly.

I had, before I wrote it, dug up all the controversies of the Reformation, and also Christian Platonism; and tried to give the Orthodox Panorama. *Without us* – the answer *and* integration of forensic justification and imputation of the righteousness of Christ; the *with us* – the inner grace, working *as* grace (in the Protestant view), and the *in us* – the answer to the

Spirit-movements, but also the Catholic idea of grace in a certain way.

The last essay I wrote at Christmas, and the cancer was then already bursting down upon me. So I had death very near me in my mind, and wanted to say all I could, to get it said in time! But I resurrected.

And just now I am in the throes of writing on my beloved theme: 'the foolishness'.[1] Our Greeks want a talk next Sunday, so I am in a whirlwind of thought from Socrates, prophets, St Paul, to the Baptist.

October 24th, 1973

I wrote a few pages on 'the fool' – the prophet-fool, the philosopher fool, St Paul-fool, St John Baptist-fool, and our Monastery-fool![1]

It was my last inspiration, where the prophetic mind meets the philosopher's mind precisely. It is exciting.

June 28th, 1974

I often wonder about the distilledness, whether it be fair to people, but I cannot write differently, because it is a thing which has to be *lived* by each one in his very own way and cannot be passed on directly. We are *not* pastoral in the obvious sense; let alone missionary. Our teaching must remain indirect to the last painful consequence.

June 29th, 1974

The Fool and *The Realism* are the two pieces of writing I achieved lately, and they follow on to the last two essays of *Orthodox Potential* and come to you as a sign that we will never 'go away'. They broke straight out of my heart, when I was still wholly living inside the region of death (and inside I am still), and there, in the end, I saw the world as a forest of crosses, rising up on every infinitesimal point from hell to heaven, linking them inseparably, for ever, together: the Kingdom of Heaven, and we cannot escape it. I feel such an immense desire, quickly, quickly, to pass on to you all that I am and have. A very great joy is in me. One might say that it

---

[1] *The Fool* (unpublished). Cf. II, November 22nd, 1973 (p. 20)

is unfair to write so short and distilled, but I feel I have no time nor strength left for more, and also that it must be *lived* in some form by each one in the way which accords with the person. But I feel it to be relevant, that those who can bear it, should, because there is so great a cry in the world for comfort – and only the fools can go to the root of the grief.

July 2nd, 1974
More and more I adhere to my 'battlehorse' of the double movement (*Eastern Spirituality*); i.e. what happens inside the realm of the Spirit is at the same time temporal and eternal, and therefore never merely past and also not-from-eternity. Therefore a sudden and total recognition is natural although it fills us also with an ineffable joy and wonder. There is no question of accepting or not from our side: it *is*. What now remains is carefully to follow and listen to the 'footsteps' of the Spirit; he will show how to solve the practical things. They always follow lovingly and tenderly the Spirit. I insist that matter and body love the Spirit and rejoice to follow.

December 6th, 1974
... and in *Sceptrum Regale* (1960), I found for the first time my innermost integration. It is my love-song; in the outward non-fulfilment; and inward total fulfilment.

December 12th, 1974 [to Father Ralph]
Back to the *Sceptrum Regale*. I there defined our existence as our being-loved-of-God, and this is the open centre, and our innermost core, and for us monks the emphatic joy of being a monk, that we are granted to put the total weight of our life into that unmarred and unspoilable reality, which is not real and non-real, as all our earthly conditions, but *only* real; and from here comes the fearlessness towards both doubt and emotional upset, because, however heavy, the centre of our existence *can* not be touched or determined by it, because it is God himself, God's desert in man, his solitude and infinitely tender waiting for our attention – and speechless excitement at his presence.
    Now this fits precisely my other three diagrams of my last years. Only these are more sharply drawn, and should be

seen together with the tenderness of the centre. The End-point, the gap, the contiguous lines are all wider explications of the centre; and from the purely personal widening out over the whole.

The End-point (*Eastern Spirituality*) could now be seen as the fountain of love for us, and shows the toppling over of the 'middle sphere' into the transcendent centre. Christ, tall and wholly still, and we rushing towards him *with* – not without – our love for each other; with any muddle or not muddle, but warm, not 'detached'. It is the only thing we can do for each other, to throw the other into that presence and over the brink; and the joy of the monk is to do this in wider measure – to love more intensely, not less. And indiscriminately, not carefully and anxiously. Fill up the whole soul and busily carry it to the End-point, into the stillness of breaking eternity. One could call it intercession, but I mean a living activity, a total commitment. Love is not a commandment, it is the highest privilege of the monk, but not an 'aseptic' love.

Now, what I mean is (with a little training of sacrificing claims of 'fulfilment') to meet people and go straight to their centre; as monks we may jump across the middle sphere – socially, pastorally, personally, we are uncommitted (I mean as desert monks) – and see the other wholly in his being loved. This is not the same as 'loving Christ in the other', a concept I will not accept. It is too cheap and leads to the irreality of an idealism.

But in jumping across the middle sphere it does of course mean that we must carry and 'see' and accept it, our own *and* the other's. I had some training in that, as you will imagine!! Carry it tenderly, and yet never give it reality, hardly even so much as considering it worthy of correcting. It will run down like an unwound clock if it meets with no response. This does, of course, only work inside the monastic training, if the disciple has his will firmly set on the transcendent end; but it must work always, one way or another, and it makes the soul grow and brings joy. Because it is, as far as we can live it, the life of the saints in heaven. I see that always as a passing freely through each other without any hindrance.

The only thing we can mar is the vision for ourselves, and

the access towards the centre for ourselves. This, of course, is heavy, but never final, because Christ *is*.

If one takes the second diagram of *the gap* (Jordan in the Baptism ikon, the cleft rock in the Christmas ikon, the gates of hell in Christ's descent into hell) to relate it with the centre, the being-loved-of-God which is our life, is the Cross raised high in the gap; the presence of active love at the centre of the world, and the world's history and human thinking, where it touches its limit and is at the brink into eternity.

And then the contiguous lines, where I saw the world as a forest of crosses, each infinitesimal particle of world at the End-point every instant, linked by the Cross, the centre, the being infinitely loved, with eternity, from hell to heaven. And once one sees it one would never – if one is allowed to be one – be anything else but a monk, to use every breath of one's life as a silent witness to the attention, to the infinitely being-loved which makes one's own heart bubble over; and nothing else matters.

But again, one hits one's head, ever and ever, at one's own limitation of all sorts; only it does not matter, getting lost in the middle sphere in a thousand ways and not-ways, and only, perhaps, on a very restricted small space can we achieve some of it. But the proportions are strangely dispropor-tionate. The tiniest attempt of pure love proves more and, looking back, is amazing in forward movement and generat-ing more freedom.

Love on earth *can* only prove itself in sacrifice, if Christ himself could not do it otherwise. And the following crea-tively – as he told us to do precisely as he, only ridiculously small and never quite purely – but never passively.

If one rules out any notion of passive redemption, and sees the following as wholly a struggle of freedom to 'see' what *is* and what is love, things grip one forever and there is no hindrance anywhere. Any evil becomes a field of action and work – or of repentance – forward.

March 17th, 1975
I will not wait any longer till I can write properly on a very dear theme of the universal incarnation; the self-limitation of God in the transference of his Spirit and his self-

communication to us, the *causa prima* and *causa finalis* of every
movement of thought and of event. But I will just tell you
that I still live, and who knows, perhaps still at 'the beginning' of the last passage. Your letter was to me an immense
joy. My pamphlet[1] and last clarification on the dialectic
approach to spiritual things, without which I could never
approach the Gospel, nor my own death (which is, of course,
now ever in my thought, though there may be a long stretch
still of yet more reduced movability) will come this week and
I shall send you a copy. In order to keep the line uncluttered it
is in as few words as possible, but it holds, *in nuce*, all I can
think of in the end, and, especially the universalization of the
last diagram – the linking of hell to heaven and the infinitesimal communication which is our existence.

June 6th, 1975 [in hospital]
I took the *Brothers Karamasov* with me to read, just to see
what it was that in them, in my tender youth, was so forceful
to direct my whole life, make me a nurse, made me
Orthodox, lifted me out of a stifling piousity when I was
growing up, and a futile morality code. And now I am deeply
impressed, what slender passages these were ... a dream, a
vision, of no personal impact to him, yet Spirit-bearing,
lightening, and I see what strange things books are when they
go out; they have a sort of life wholly of their own, they act,
inspire, far beyond the author's conception and *without* him.
A strange proof of the Holy Spirit's working.

June 10th, 1975
Reading my Dostoievsky I am deeply impressed what a
slight word, a slight vision of his, which for him may have
meant next to nothing, and was nothing more than an
ingenious thrust of the pen, one slight paragraph, could raise
such a storm of redirection, of solution, of foundation to my
life. What a mysterious working of words in the writing.
Almost they work outside the author on their own, like in an
operation theatre, the table prepared and the instruments; and
one small cut. So God seems to make use of books unpredict-
ably.

[1] *The Realism of the Orthodox Faith*

July 19th, 1975
Don't worry about being 'slow', I have not yet found anyone who, being quick, has understood me. And I have ever taken care to write so, that reading means an active re-creating of the thought, in your own way, form and rhythm. I should hate to impose my thought on anyone. It would be futile and boring.

October 17th, 1975
With reading, I am in a strange condition. As if I had no more time, and then I turn away, although I want to read. This inner turning away, against my own desire, is so strong, and all so much unseen, turning into that total uncertainty, that life which cannot be grasped nor foreseen, and yet my whole soul is concentrated intensely on to what I can in no way grasp. Only I rejoice in what a degree, and so wholly, I am able to say, that the Platonic attitude, in the Christian faith, is more and more totally confirmed and a carrying, so deeply satisfying source and joy in the immediate face of death; and I never know why it is so difficult for others to grasp it; perhaps it rules out too much of self-importance, and does not satisfy the fighting instincts!! But I rejoice in this ultimate grace of 'witness'. It was perhaps true that my innermost task was to live it, instead of repeating what Gauss taught. And by living I perhaps did go a few steps further – but this is hard to teach because it can so easily be misunderstood. My three diagrams, thought into one, are perhaps nearest to expressing it – but who understands them? In writing we are now going to show the bridges to the Orthodox texts, which will, of course, be a strong reinforcement and also exciting.

April 6th, 1976
Just for historical reasons I am sending you my thesis. It has many Cudworth texts which are interesting, because one can so easily see the direct connection from theology to philosophy – and how precisely the unity of mind and heart work in a Platonist. The third chapter – 'The Criterion of Truth' – is the most important for myself. The fourth chapter could have been a lot better, if I had had more time; but it can be

filled up with the essay[1] and the article.[2] As always I worked completely independently, digesting that monstrous book – for as a book it is a monster – in thought with finest connections.

September 21st, 1977
It [*The Realism of the Orthodox Faith*] is the last 'vision' of what I saw in a blaze of joy thirty years ago, when I delved into *Evil in the New Testament* and further, *The Hidden Treasure*, *Sceptrum Regale*, and the last two essays in *Orthodox Potential*. So it grew through the years, and as it grew I found it in our liturgical texts and the ikons fully and precisely and in ineffable joy.

Adam tripped up, fell and was crushed and deceived of the ancient hope of becoming like God. But he rises, made like God indeed by union with the Word, and by suffering is given immunity from passions, and, as the Son who sits upon the throne with the Father and the Spirit, is glorified (Matins Canon, Sunday, Tone 1, Ode 6).

[1] *Ralph Cudworth: Mystical Thinker*
[2] 'Ralph Cudworth', in *The Month*, June 1976